MAR   2010

W9-CJQ-449

History of
THE ANCIENT AND MEDIEVAL WORLD

SECOND EDITION

VOLUME 7

SOUTHERN AND EASTERN ASIA

Marshall Cavendish
Reference
New York

Marshall Cavendish
99 White Plains Road
Tarrytown, New York 10591

www.marshallcavendish.us

© 2009 Marshall Cavendish Corporation

Library of Congress Cataloging-in-Publication Data

History of the ancient and medieval world / [edited by Henk Dijkstra]. -- 2nd ed.
   v. cm.
   Includes bibliographical references and index.
   Contents: v. 1. The first civilizations -- v. 2. Western Asia and the Mediterranean -- v. 3. Ancient Greece -- v. 4. The Roman Empire -- v. 5. The changing shape of Europe -- v. 6. The early Middle Ages in western Asia and Europe -- v. 7. Southern and eastern Asia -- v. 8. Europe in the Middle Ages -- v. 9. Western Asia, northern Europe, and Africa in the Middle Ages -- v. 10. The passing of the medieval world -- v. 11. Index.
   ISBN 978-0-7614-7789-1 (set) -- ISBN 978-0-7614-7791-4 (v. 1) -- ISBN 978-0-7614-7792-1 (v. 2) -- ISBN 978-0-7614-7793-8 (v. 3) -- ISBN 978-0-7614-7794-5 (v. 4) -- ISBN 978-0-7614-7795-2 (v. 5) -- ISBN 978-0-7614-7796-9 (v. 6) -- ISBN 978-0-7614-7797-6 (v. 7) -- ISBN 978-0-7614-7798-3 (v. 8) -- ISBN 978-0-7614-7799-0 (v. 9) -- ISBN 978-0-7614-7800-3 (v. 10) -- ISBN 978-0-7614-7801-0 (v. 11)
   1. History, Ancient. 2. Middle Ages. 3. Civilization, Medieval. I. Dijkstra, Henk.
   D117.H57 2009
   940.1--dc22
                                  2008060052

Printed in Malaysia

12 11 10 09 08 7 6 5 4 3 2 1

General Editor: Henk Dijkstra

Marshall Cavendish
Project Editor: Brian Kinsey
Publisher: Paul Bernabeo
Production Manager: Michael Esposito

Brown Reference Group
Project Editor: Chris King
Text Editors: Shona Grimbly, Charles Phillips
Designer: Lynne Lennon
Cartographers: Joan Curtis, Darren Awuah
Picture Researcher: Laila Torsun
Indexer: Christine Michaud
Managing Editor: Tim Cooke

PICTURE CREDITS

SET CONTENTS

VOLUME CONTENTS

THE EARLY HISTORY OF CHINA

At the start of recorded history, several different early human cultures developed in parallel in various parts of China. They were united for the first time around 2200 BCE, and in 221 BCE, they were formally bound together by the first emperor.

The first people appeared in China around 2 million years ago. Known as *Homo erectus*, they are the ancestors of modern humans. It is uncertain whether *Homo erectus* originated in Africa and spread out around the world or whether the earliest humans developed independently in Africa and Asia. *Homo erectus* had a smaller brain than the modern human but differed from the ape by walking upright rather than on all fours. *Homo erectus* was the first humanoid species to use fire and to live in caves.

The *Homo erectus* remains that were found in 1927 CE in caves at Zhoukoudian became known as Peking Man—after the former English name for the nearest city, Beijing. The remains, dated to around 460,000 years ago, show that Peking Man used implements made of rock and animal bones, hunted and ate animals, and lived communally in caves.

The first farmers

For many thousands of years, early humans lived in China as hunter-gatherers. The *Homo erectus* species was gradually superseded by modern humans (*Homo sapiens*). Then, between around 7000 and 5000 BCE, people living along the Hwang He (Hwang Ho; Yellow River) in central China began to settle in small, semipermanent villages and to live primarily by agriculture.

People of the Yang-shao culture (c. 5000–2000 BCE) farmed millet, wheat, and rice; some kept goats, sheep, pigs, dogs, and cattle and experimented with cultivating silkworms. They also hunted wild animals and fished in the Yellow River and its tributaries. They lived in single-room wattle-and-daub houses with thatched roofs, sunken floors, and central hearths. They made pottery painted in red, white, and black with geometric decorations as well as figurative images of animals and human faces. They had not yet developed the use of the pottery wheel.

The Yang-shao people are named after the first village of the culture, uncovered in 1921 CE in Henan (Honan) Province; they also lived in Shanxi (Shan-hsi) Province. Some of them used a slash-and-burn method of agriculture. In this technique, a forested area was partially cleared with sickles before the remaining vegetation was burned; the field was then used for one to five years before it was abandoned and a new area was cleared. Other Yang-shao farmers used permanent fields. They worked with polished-stone tools and are thus classified as belonging to the Neolithic period (the New Stone Age).

The Stone Age is so named because people used tools made of stone rather than the metal tools (made from bronze

or iron) that their descendants would use. In the Paleolithic period (the Old Stone Age), people used chipped-stone tools, whereas in the Neolithic period, people used polished-stone tools. During the Neolithic Revolution, people in many parts of the world started to use polished-stone tools and to abandon their nomadic hunter-gatherer lifestyle, settling instead in farming villages.

Expert potters

Another important Chinese Neolithic civilization was the Long-shan (Lung-shan) culture (c. 2000–1850 BCE) in the central and lower parts of the Yellow

This bronze food vessel was forged in the 12th century BCE during the Shang dynasty.

CHINA DURING THE ZHOU PERIOD

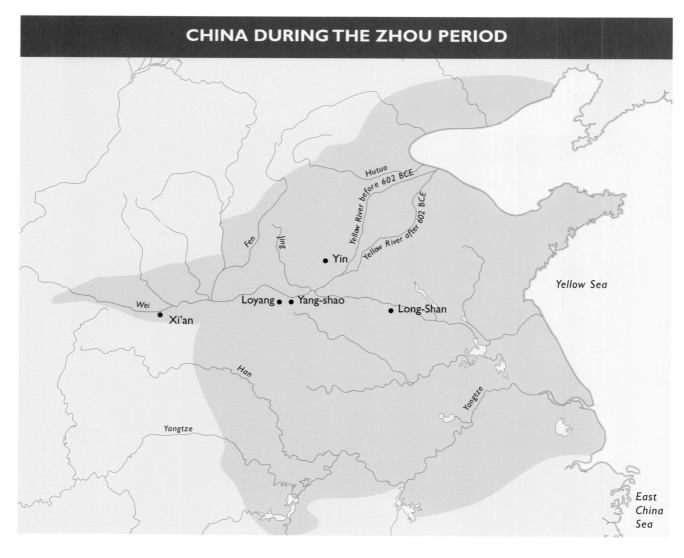

KEY

Area under Zhou control by 481 BCE

River Valley. The Long-shan culture may have derived from that of the Yang-shao, but it is usually considered independent. It takes its name from a village in Shandong (Shantung) Province, the first settlement of its type to be excavated. Long-shan people lived in much the same way as the Yang-shao. They developed the use of the pottery wheel and produced highly polished black containers known as eggshell pots. Their villages were more permanent than those of the Yang-shao, and they were surrounded by mud walls and sometimes by moats. Such structures were clearly fortifications, and archaeologists have found stone spear-tips and arrowheads in Long-shan vil-lages. The Long-shan probably practiced fortune-telling through the interpreta-tion of animal bones; the diviner would heat tortoise shells or other skeletal remains and use the resulting pattern of cracks to predict the future or divine the will of the gods.

The Bronze Age

By around 2000 BCE, roughly contem-poraneously with the Long-shan culture, people on the banks of the Huang-pu River (near modern Shanghai) started working copper and making bronze objects. Chinese people were also carv-ing jade, the country's main precious stone, into miniature axes and rings.

Soon, a social elite emerged; within settlements of the period, archaeologists have excavated sizeable clay platforms, which were the foundations of large buildings erected by those rich or powerful enough to mobilize a workforce.

Around 2200 BCE, China's first ruling dynasty, the Xia (Hsia), was established, traditionally by Yu the Great. Archaeologists have searched Long-shan sites for evidence of the Xia dynasty but without success; Yu and his descendants are generally regarded as mythical figures. However, legend gives way to verifiable history in the era of the successors to the Xia, the rulers of the Shang dynasty.

The Shang dynasty

The Shang dynasty ruled in the valley of the Yellow River from around 1766 to 1050 BCE. The Shang kings had several different capitals, the most celebrated of which was the last at Yin (modern Anyang in Henan Province), where they established themselves in 1384 BCE.

In the Shang era, the Chinese began to build cities, and archaeologists have excavated palaces, temples, and the graves of the social elite in and around those cities. Shang society was hierarchical, with a wealthy aristocracy and rule by a hereditary monarch. Most of the people were poor farmers who grew millet, wheat, barley, and rice as well as raising sheep, oxen, pigs, and dogs. The rulers appointed by the king were the masters of the farms, the landed estates, and the villages surrounding the cities. The elite had access to bronze objects and placed

This is the reconstructed skull of Peking Man, an early human who lived in China around 460,000 years ago.

them in their graves (see box, page 876), but the majority still lived as their ancestors had lived in the Stone Age, using wooden spades and stone sickles. The poor people's earthenware was rough, while their masters' was delicate and ornate.

A literate priestly class was responsible for matters of religion. The priests' main duties were to divine the future by interpreting bone oracles and to channel advice from a panel of deities headed by Shang Di (Shang Ti; the Lord on High). The Shang people worshipped their ancestors as well as their gods, sacrificing both humans and animals to them. The priests were also expected to keep records. Tens of thousands of oracular writings of the period have been preserved, and it is because of those records that so much more is known about the late Shang period (c. 1250–1050 BCE) than about the earlier Shang period.

The divination records are the oldest texts in the Chinese language. Chinese writing uses a single character for every word, and there are more than 40,000 characters altogether. Some 3,000 characters from the Shang dynasty have been identified, incised on tortoiseshells and on the scapulae (shoulder blades) of the cattle and sheep that were used as oracles in divination ceremonies. Around 800 of them have been deciphered with certainty. Chinese writing has since undergone many changes, but its basic structure and many of its symbols remain unaltered.

The Zhou dynasty

According to traditional accounts, the Zhou (Chou) took control of China around 1050 BCE and subjugated the

THE XINJIANG MUMMIES

More than 100 naturally preserved bodies, dating from as long ago as 2000 BCE, have been found in the Xinjiang region of northwestern China. The corpses, the first of which was discovered in 1978 CE, had avoided decomposition through burial in the hot, dusty soil between the Celestial Mountains (Tian Shan) and the Taklimakan Desert.

The mummies have Caucasian rather than Asiatic facial features, dark-brown or yellow-blond hair, and long limbs. They were all buried with patterned woven cloth, and some graves contained wagon wheels. Made of three carved boards fastened with dowels, the wheels are virtually identical to wheels made in Ukraine, on the plains of eastern Europe. The people were seemingly either travelers from Europe or the descendants of Europeans.

Scholars have debated the significance of the finds. Some historians suggest that the bodies are the remains of raiders or nomads; others contend that Caucasian people were actually typical of the population in the area at the time (c. 2000–1000 BCE) and that East Asian peoples arrived there only after around 1000 BCE. Some ancient Chinese texts describe encounters with tall blond people; scholars had previously dismissed such accounts as imaginary, but the Xinjiang mummies compelled them to reconsider.

Today, most inhabitants of the area are Uyghurs, a Turkic people who are also resident in several of the states that border modern China, notably Kazakhstan, Kyrgyzstan, and Pakistan, as well as in Uzbekistan. Some Uyghurs want to establish an independent state of their own, East Turkestan (also known as Uyghurstan).

This is one of the 4,000-year-old mummies that were unearthed at Xinjiang in the late 20th century CE. The facial features are notably non-Asiatic.

Shang. The Zhou lived in the valley of the Wei River in the far west of China. They belonged to a different ethnic group from the Shang, although they shared the same bronze culture. The traditional Chinese account describes the last Shang king as a degenerate monster whose replacement by the Zhou was the will of heaven; the Shang's heavenly mandate to rule had been passed on to the Zhou. The same justification for the seizure of power had previously been used to legitimize the Shang replacement of the Xia. Thereafter, such explanations became standard every time there was a change of dynasty.

The Zhou ruled most of northern China, including the fertile banks of the Yangtze River. Their domain was so extensive and communication was so limited that they delegated administrative tasks to hereditary vassals. Each lord ruled over designated territory that he controlled with his own army. Agricultural lands were divided into squares of nine plots; peasant families worked the outer eight tracts as their own land and collectively farmed the central tract for their lord. Below peasants in social order were domestic slaves.

The lords in each state were nominally subordinate to the dynastic king, who was said to rule by mandate from heaven, but in reality the lords became more powerful than the king. They frequently warred with each other, and the victors seized the territory of the vanquished. Through a process of consolidation, the states became larger, fewer in number, and increasingly autonomous, forcing the king to share power with the lords. Eventually, the king was no more than a symbolic head of these states.

On the periphery of China, states formed alliances with non-Chinese groups. In 770 BCE, an alliance of several states and non-Chinese forces drove the Zhou to establish a new capital in the

east at Loyang. The rulers from this period are thus known as the Eastern Zhou. They had little control over their dependent states.

During this period, the chariot—for so long central to the conduct of war—was replaced by infantry as the main instrument of war. Farmers were forced to serve in the infantry and came under increasingly direct control even when they were not mobilized.

From the fifth century BCE, a regular army became essential to China as the country was called on to resist recurring incursions from the north and west. The frequency of the attacks increased greatly in the fourth century BCE, when nomads from the steppes of central Asia attacked Chinese farmers time and again. In an effort to defend the Chinese people against such raids, the rulers of the

This ax, made of jade, was used for ceremonies in the 18th century BCE, during the early Shang dynasty.

THE EXCAVATION OF ANYANG

The late Shang capital of Yin (Yinxu) at modern Anyang in Henan Province was excavated between 1927 and 1936 CE. Yin was a major city that, at its peak around 1250–1050 BCE, extended for 3.6 miles (5.8 km) along the Huan River and included a wealth of palaces, temples, and royal graves.

All but one of the royal graves of Yin had been plundered. The exception was the tomb of Fu Hao, queen of the 21st Shang king, Wu Ding (Wu Ting; ruled 1250–1192 BCE). Her grave was found to contain more than 3,500 pounds (1,600 kg) of bronze pieces; around 600 items of carved stone, jade, and bone; nearly 7,000 cowrie shells (then used as currency); 16 human skeletons (presumably attendants); and 6 dog skeletons. Other graves at Anyang contained evidence of similarly grand burials, including mass interments of people and animals (monkeys, deer, horses, and even elephants) and the oldest chariots in China. The bronze vessels in the Anyang graves originally contained offerings of food and wine for the spirits of ancestors. In addition, the graves included a collection of oracle bones, which are of particular importance because, during the Shang dynasty, the questions posed by diviners and the answers received from heaven were recorded for the first time on the bones, making them a form of early historical text. Before the Anyang finds, Chinese script was thought to have developed from Sumerian and ancient Egyptian writing, but it is now known to have evolved independently.

This four-legged wine vessel, dating from around 1300 to 1030 BCE, was one of the treasures discovered during the excavation of Anyang.

Zhou era built long walls, usually of clay, along their northern and western frontiers. They also erected defensive walls between the various states.

The states made alliances with each other against the invaders. Such treaties among the individual states provided them with the political stability that they needed as the power of the Zhou dynasty began to wane during the seventh and sixth centuries BCE. However, by the late fifth century BCE, most of the alliances among the states had failed. The era of civil conflict and anarchy that ensued—known as the Period of the Warring States (c. 475–221 BCE)—overlaps with the final centuries of the Zhou dynasty, which continued as the ruling dynasty until its collapse in 256 BCE.

The late Zhou period was a time of enormous significance in Chinese economic and political development. Despite the conflict and unrest, the era was prosperous. The Bronze Age gave way to the Iron Age, as iron tools and weapons, first introduced into China around 500 BCE, became commonplace. A market economy emerged that was based on coins. China's first laws were written. An administrative system was set up that allowed government to undertake large-scale public works such as the construction of river dykes, irrigation works, and canals. The population expanded as farming became far more productive, largely as a result of vast irrigation projects.

However, despite the new prosperity, life remained very hard for many people. Farmers were still often victims of war, whether as soldiers or noncombatants, and had to pay exorbitant taxes; epi-

This oracle bone was inscribed in the 14th or 13th century BCE. Artifacts such as this display the earliest extant examples of Chinese script.

demics, floods, and famine still brought periodic devastation. Many farmers, having fallen on hard times, were forced to sell their children in order to survive or had to accept work as laborers on grand projects such as an ostentatious grave for a member of the aristocracy.

The final years of the Zhou dynasty also saw an extraordinary flowering of philosophy in China. The two main stimuli were Confucius and Lao-tzu, sixth-century-BCE thinkers whose teachings gave rise to the philosophical and religious programs of Confucianism and Taoism.

The first emperor

In 221 BCE, the northwestern feudal state of Qin (Ch'in), which was richer and militarily stronger than its neighbors, seized the royal power that Chinese states had warred over since 500 BCE. The king of Qin, influenced by the work of the philosopher Shang Yang (c. 390–338 BCE), declared himself Shi Huang Di (Shi Huang Ti), or first emperor of the Qin dynasty. The Chinese called their country either by the name of its current ruling dynasty or Zhongguot (Chung-kuo; the Middle Kingdom), which reflected their perception of themselves as being at the center of the world. Eventually, the name *China*—a variation of Qin—was adopted by the rest of the world as the permanent name of the country, regardless of its ruler.

The Qin regime adopted the philosophy of legalism, one of the fundamental tenets of which was that people are naturally evil and therefore need to be ruled by a strong king, army, and administration. The first emperor of China imposed a centralized administration on the semiautonomous feudal states that had existed before his accession. He broke up the lands of aristocratic families into

THE LONG RIVER

The Yangtze River is the longest natural waterway in China and Asia, flowing 3,400 miles (5,470 km) from the Kunlun Mountains in southwest Qinghai (Tsinghai) Province, south through Sichuan (Szechwan) Province into Yunnan (Yün-nan) Province, then northeast and east across central China to the East China Sea, just north of Shanghai. The Chinese name for the river is Chang Jiang (Ch'ang Chiang), meaning "Long River"; in Chinese, the name *Yangtze* refers only to the last 400 miles (644 km) of the river's course, where it flows through the region of the 10th-century-BCE Yang kingdom.

The river drains more than 650,000 square miles (1,683,500 km^2) of China through its numerous tributaries. Its main branches are the Han, the

The Yangtze River is China's larder. This photograph shows an angler in search of one of the river's abundant freshwater fish species and rice cultivation on the terraced hillsides on the banks.

Yalong (Ya-lung), the Jialing (Chia-ling), the Min, the Tuo He (T'o Ho), the Wu, and the Huang He (Huang Ho; Yellow River).

The regions around China's great rivers are the most populous and economically productive areas of the country. The Yangtze is navigable by seagoing ships for 600 miles (965 km) from its mouth and by river steamers for 1,000 miles (1,609 km), but passage through the Yangtze Gorges is perilous for boats. With its tributaries, the river is a great fertilizer of the land. Chinese civilization, based on agriculture, originated in the great river valleys. The Huang He derives its English name from the large quantity of yellow clay it carries. This clay or silt is loess, a fertile loam, and each flooding of the river leaves a layer of loess on the land, greatly increasing its fertility. The Yangtze deposits more than 6 billion cubic feet (168 million m^3) of silt annually in Jiangsu Province alone, helping the region to be a major area of rice production.

provinces and assigned bureaucrats to run them. He encouraged private land-holding. The situation of the farmers did not improve much. Those who now received the land as private property were members of the privileged classes. They controlled the system of taxation and lobbied for influence at court.

The first emperor built the Great Wall of China, which combined long stretch-es of preexisting defensive walls into a single, vast, continuous barrier. During the course of his reign, the emperor added around 1,200 miles (1,930 km) to the frontier defenses. When the wall was completed in 204 BCE, it extended for 4,160 miles (6,700 km) along the coun-try's northern and eastern frontiers. The use of forced labor to achieve this con-struction feat later became a popular cause of resentment.

In addition, the first emperor ruth-lessly expanded his territory. He forced peasants into military service and dis-patched his armies south to the Yuan Hong (Yüan Hung; the Red River in modern Vietnam). He took control of the enormous area covered by the mod-ern provinces of Sichuan (Szechwan), Yunnan (Yün-nan), and Guizhou (Kuei-chou), as well as all of China north of the Yangtze River, including parts of the Korean Peninsula.

Under Shi Huang Di, the Qin regime promoted economic and social integra-tion across this vast empire, imposing standardized coinage, weights, measures, and culture. Shi Huang Di also simplified written Chinese. He tried to impose the philosophy of legalism on all his domains, and in 213 BCE, he ordered the infamous burning of the books, in which all written documents except works of history, divination, agriculture, and medicine were cast into the flames. He brooked no opposition, even in phi-losophy; no fewer than 460 scholars were executed during his reign.

The first emperor was also obsessed with the idea of an elixir that could bring eternal youth. In 219 BCE, following the guidance of his diviners, he sent 3,000 of his young subjects on a mission across the Eastern Sea in search of a legendary Land of the Immortals. None of the explorers returned. Many years later, legends arose suggesting that the lost youths had discovered the islands of Japan and settled there.

The authority and the organizational skills of the first emperor are apparent in his vast burial mound near the modern city of Xi'an. The earthworks at the site

This 17th-century-CE woodcut is an idealized portrait of Shi Huang Di, the first emperor of China (ruled 221–210 BCE).

measure around one-third of a mile (500 m) in diameter. Inside them was an underground reconstruction of China, including re-creations of the Yangtze River, the Yellow River, and the starry heavens dotted with pearls. In 1974 CE, while digging a water well around 1,000 yards (1 km) to the east of the tomb, local farmers discovered four pits containing a buried terra-cotta army, comprising more than 8,000 life-size statues of soldiers with their horses. The figures were arrayed in military formation, ready to defend the emperor in the afterlife.

The Han dynasty

The Qin empire remained in the hands of its founding family for only 15 years. This short reign is testimony, perhaps, to

Parts of the Great Wall of China still remain as imposing as they were when the entire structure was completed in 204 BCE.

the fact that its basic philosophy of legalism had not gained general acceptance. Following the death of the first emperor in 210 BCE, the Chinese rebelled. After a series of popular uprisings, Liu Bang (Liu Pang), an army officer of nonaristocratic birth, proclaimed the new Han dynasty in 206 BCE. The Han dynasty held power for more than four centuries, until 220 CE. Its emperors retained the centralized system of state administration established by the Qin but rejected most other aspects of their predecessors' legalism. Instead, the rulers of the Han dynasty later adopted Confucianism as the underlying philosophy of the bureaucracy that they developed to organize their vast empire.

The terra-cotta warriors originally held wooden spears, but their weaponry disintegrated during the 2,000 years between interment and rediscovery.

See also:

China's Imperial Dynasties (volume 7, page 894) • Early Chinese Thinkers (volume 7, page 882)

EARLY CHINESE THINKERS

TIME LINE

c. 570 BCE

Birth of Lao-tzu.

551 BCE

Birth of Kongqiu, known in West as Confucius.

c. 490 BCE

Death of Lao-tzu.

479 BCE

Death of Confucius.

c. 475 BCE

Period of the Warring States begins.

c. 371 BCE

Birth of Confucian philosopher Mencius.

221 BCE

Period of the Warring States ends; start of Qin dynasty.

213 BCE

Qin adopt legalism as state philosophy.

206 BCE

Establishment of Han dynasty.

136 BCE

Han replace legalism with Confucianism.

c. 100 BCE

First Chinese historical work, Shih-chi, written.

The sixth century BCE saw the birth in China of two great philosophers—Confucius and Lao-tzu. Their works would have a great influence on later Chinese history and be read throughout much of southern and eastern Asia.

The late years of the Zhou (Chou) dynasty, between the sixth and the third centuries BCE, saw an extraordinary flowering of philosophy in China that would eventually exert a significant and lasting influence on China's neighbors throughout eastern Asia. By 480 BCE, the Zhou rulers, whose ancestors had governed since around 1050 BCE and had once held sway over a large part of China, no longer retained any real power. The country was politically fragmented, with several independent states competing for preeminence. Constant warfare, with its attendant confusion and insecurity, fostered a search for peace and order. Many Chinese people whose worldly ambitions had been thwarted turned for consolation to ideas and theories.

During this period, a number of philosophical schools formulated new ideas about individual behavior and society. The most important such school was based on the teachings of Confucius. The philosophy that later became known in English as Confucianism would ultimately become the predominant tradition throughout China, Korea, Japan, and the northern part of Southeast Asia. The nine principal books of classical Chinese philosophy were all written during this period (see box, page 887). In Chinese script, the character that means "classic"

also means "the warp of a woven cloth"; the ideas and teachings of Confucius are woven throughout those nine books.

Confucius

The man known in the West as Confucius was born Kongqiu (K'ung Ch'iu) in 551 BCE in the state of Lu. He later became known as Kong Fuzi (K'ung Fu-tzu), meaning "Grand Master Kong." Neither the name *Confucius* nor the term *Confucianism* is used in China.

In Confucius's lifetime, Chinese society was patriarchal and organized along feudal lines. Individuals were expected to dedicate themselves to serving the government. Within the government, a highly competitive literate elite was responsible for record-keeping; all education was designed to prepare individuals for this work. Heaven was believed to be the great overseer that sanctioned the rule of each dynasty and government. When rulers were ousted, their removal was taken to be in accordance with the celestial will.

Confucius's family were nobles who had fallen on hard times. The philosopher's father was a minor bureaucrat. Confucius dedicated himself to learning

The influence of Confucianism spread throughout Asia. This Japanese woodcut depicts the founder himself, Confucius.

祖述尧舜
宪章文武
上律天时
下袭水玉

刘煜敬书

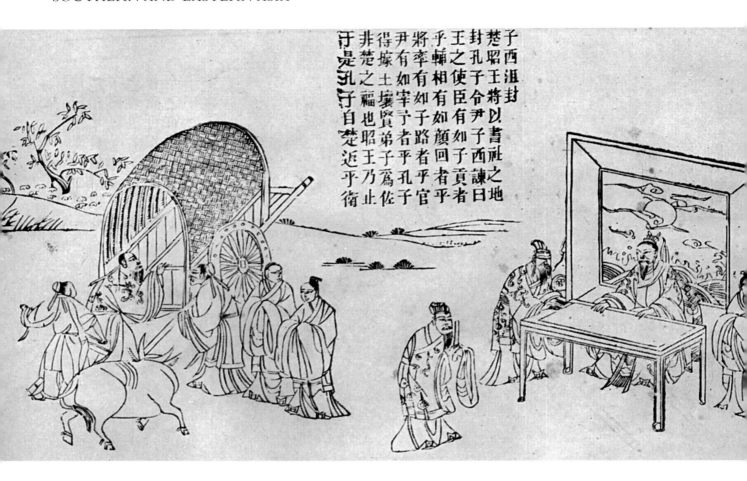

子西沮封
昭王將以書社之地
封孔子西王令尹子西諫曰
王之使臣有如子貢者乎
曰無有
王之輔相有如顏回者乎
曰無有
王之將率有如子路者乎
曰無有
王之官尹有如宰予者乎
曰無有
且楚之祖封於周
號為子男五十里
今孔丘述三五之法
明周召之業
王若用之
則楚安得世世堂堂方數千里乎
夫文王在豐
武王在鎬
百里之君
卒為天子
今孔丘得據土壤
賢弟子為佐
非楚之福也
昭王乃止
於是孔子自楚返乎衛

This undated illustration depicts Confucius riding in an ox cart, traditionally his favored mode of transportation.

and worked first as a bureaucrat and then as a teacher. He later rose to become an adviser to local leaders, a magistrate, and then a minister of justice for the state of Lu. Disillusioned with the ruling elite in Lu, because it paid little heed to his teachings, Confucius then left his home state at age 52 and traveled with a growing number of students. At age 67, he returned home to work as a teacher and writer. Confucius died at age 73 in 479 BCE. The *Lun Yu* (*Sayings of Confucius*) is traditionally attributed to the philosopher, but scholars do not know for certain which parts accurately reflect his thinking as opposed to that of his followers. Confucius was a political as well as an ethical theorist; many of his teachings have their roots in his experience as an adviser to state leaders.

Regardless of whether the *Lun Yu* was written by Confucius himself or by his acolytes, the work is definitively Confucian in content and tone. It emphasizes the need for internal and external order, which Confucius believed could be achieved through personal rectitude and respect for tradition. The *Lun Yu* looked back to an ideal society, exemplified by the early Zhou dynasty of the 11th and 10th centuries BCE, and advocated reestablishing social order through study of the rules of right conduct outlined in early Zhou literature. At that time, according to Confucius, people still followed the Tao (the Dao; the Way; the right path). Confucianism taught that studying early Zhou history would help people to rediscover the Tao and use it as a solution for their problems.

The *Lun Yu* also stresses the importance of learning. The book states: "Studying without thinking is wasted effort; thinking without studying is dangerous.... Those who have been born wise are the best people; then come those who have acquired wisdom by study; next are the ones who study to overcome their ignorance. Those who are ignorant and do not desire to study are the least of humankind.... Whoever has taken the Tao in the morning can die contented in the evening."

Confucianism assumed a fundamental hierarchy in what it regarded as the five basic human relationships. Reflecting a patriarchal society, it considered the primary relationship to be the one between ruler and subject, followed by the one between father and son, the one between husband and wife, the one between an older brother and a younger brother, and finally the one between friends.

Confucius taught that leaders should set an example of virtuous behavior for their people. According to the *Lun Yu*, he said: "He who exercises government by means of his virtue may be compared to the north polar star, which keeps its place, and all the stars turn toward it." Confucius believed that those in authority—or indeed those with the upper hand in any relationship—must never abuse their position. In the *Lun Yu*, he responds to the question "Is there a single word that can serve as a guideline for life?" as follows: "Perhaps the word is reciprocity. Never do to another what you would not wish another to do to you.... A human being who longs to occupy an important position helps another to such a position; one who wishes to succeed helps others to succeed. To judge others on the basis of what you know of yourself is the way to humanity.... Wealth and honor are what everyone desires, but if you can only

This mirror, with its nonreflective side ornately decorated with three dragons, is made of bronze and dates from the Period of the Warring States (c. 475–221 BCE). It measures slightly more than 8 inches (20.6 cm) in diameter.

obtain them by abandoning the right path, then it may be better not to have them." Confucius is also quoted as saying: "When a man departs from humanity, he no longer deserves the name."

Confucius and the Confucian philosophy inspired and codified a new concept of nobility. Previously in China, nobility had been regarded as an inborn characteristic of aristocrats only. However, for Confucius, nobility was a quality of soul that could be acquired by study, by honesty, and by living a virtuous life. He emphasized that it was possible for individuals to improve themselves and their society by cultivating their personal life. By making such efforts, anyone could become a great sage. It followed that people should be promoted to gov-

This undated illustration depicts the meeting (which may never have taken place) of Confucius (left) with the older sage Lao-tzu (seated).

ernment jobs on the basis of their ability rather than because of their birth or social standing.

Confucius attributed the misery of the warfare that was endemic in his time to a lack of nobility on the part of the rulers. He wrote: "When the personal life is cultivated, the family will be regulated; when the family is regulated, the state will be in order; and when the state is in order, there will be peace throughout the world."

Confucius's thinking was original in its rationalism and humanism. He did not deny the existence of the supernatural but believed that an appeal to it made no sense. The primary focus, he contended, should be on individual effort. His emphasis on secular human ethics was a new ideal for Chinese civilization.

Lao-tzu

Confucius's contemporary, Lao-tzu (Laozi), sought the Tao (the Dao; the Way; the supreme principle) in nature rather than in society. Very little is known of Lao-tzu's life. According to the *Shi-ji* (*Shih-chi*; *Records of the Grand Historian*)— written around 100 BCE by China's first historian, Sima Qian (Ssu-ma Ch'ien)— Lao-tzu was born around 570 BCE in what is now Hunan Province and served as an astrologer and fortune-teller at the royal Zhou court. However, many scholars doubt this biography (see box, page 889). Lao-tzu probably died around 490 BCE. From his teachings, it is clear that he examined nature to understand humanity and focused on personal growth through cultivation of inner calm and a pure mind.

The *Tao Te Ching* (*Dao De Jing*; *Classic of the Way and Its Virtue*), which explains this philosophy, is traditionally attributed to Lao-tzu but was probably recorded by his students from the things he said. The book advises people to cultivate *wu-wei* (nonaction), meaning that they should allow the Way to take its course. The

THE FIVE CLASSICS AND THE FOUR BOOKS

The *Wu Jing* (*Wu Ching*; Five Classics) are five texts dated to the Zhou (Chou) dynasty (c. 600–500 BCE). According to tradition, they were edited or written by Confucius himself. The *I Ching* (*Yi Jing*; *Book of Changes*) is a divination manual. The *Shi Jing* (*Shih Ching*; *Classic of Poetry*) is a collection of 305 court songs, hymns, and folk songs. The *Li Ji* (*Li Chi*; *Classic of Rites*) is a manual of court ceremonies and social behavior. The *Shu Jing* (*Shu Ching*; *Classic of History*) is a collection of documents reputedly written by early Zhou rulers. The *Lin Jing* (*Chun Qiu*; *Spring and Autumn Annals*) is a history of Confucius's native state of Lu for 722 to 479 BCE.

The *Si Shu* (*Ssu Shu*; Four Books) are four Confucian texts from the same period that were published in a single volume in 1190 CE (around 1,700 years after Confucius's lifetime) by the celebrated neo-Confucian scholar Chu Hsi. The first book is *Da Xue* (*Ta Hsüeh*; *Great Learning*), which gives an account of the links between a ruler's personal integrity and good government. The second is *Zong Yong* (*Chung Yung*; *The Doctrine of the Mean*), which investigates spiritual beings and the Tao. The third is the *Lun Yu* (*The Sayings of Confucius*), which supposedly contains direct quotations from Confucius recorded by his students. The last is the *Meng Zi* (*Meng-tzu*; *Mencius*), a record of the teachings of the Confucian disciple and scholar Mencius (c. 371–289 BCE). Both *Great Learning* and *The Doctrine of the Mean* are also part of one of the Five Classics—*Classic of Rites*.

Chinese students are introduced to Confucian literature by studying the Four Books, which were the basis of Chinese civil service entrance examinations for almost six centuries, from 1313 to 1905 CE. More advanced students proceed to study the Five Classics.

A Chinese woman practices divination using coins held over an edition of the I Ching.

This portrait of Lao-tzu, the founder of Taoism, is by a medieval Chinese artist.

Lao-tzu was aware that his teaching was difficult for some people to grasp. The *Tao Te Ching* states: "When the best kind of people learn the Way, then they are able, with dedication, to put it into practice. When average people are told of the Way, they can retain some things, but they forget the others. When the lowest kind of people hear of the Way, they laugh loudly at it. If they do not laugh at it, then it cannot be the Way."

Non-action needed to be cultivated in allowing the Way to flow and in trusting it to find the right course, for it could be difficult to understand where the Way was leading. As the *Tao Te Ching* puts it: "The light Way seems dark; the Way that leads forward seems to lead backward."

The teachings of Lao-tzu are referred to as Taoism (Daoism). Following Lao-tzu's advice, many Taoists (Daoists) withdrew from active life to rural retreats, where they cultivated mental tranquility and tried to find wisdom; their aim, ultimately, was to have a mystical experience of nature that would bring them into harmony with the Way.

The ideals of Taoism were in opposition to the teachings of Confucianism. Where Confucianism offered guidance on how to live well in society and how to behave ethically, Taoism appeared to advocate withdrawal from society, even from activity. In contrast to the Confucians, followers of Taoism did not believe in the effectiveness of study: "Those who study hard increase every day. Those who have understood the Way decrease every day. They decrease and decrease until they reach the point where they do nothing."

However, following the Tao is not equivalent to idleness. As the *Tao Te Ching* notes of those who have understood the Way: "They do nothing and yet nothing remains undone." As the book also states, "Only the Way is good in beginning things and good in bringing

book says: "Do nothing and all things are done." The ideal form of action, according to Lao-tzu, is not to try to think and do what is right, but to try to think and do nothing—what he calls the "doing of non-doing."

Lao-tzu emphasized a return to the simple agrarian life, a life not regulated by government. He urged rulers and government officials to avoid getting too involved in the trappings of power and in their actions: "When someone wishes to rule the world, he must be detached, because if he is drawn to object he will be unfit to rule the world."

LEGENDS OF LAO-TZU

There are many legends but few hard facts about the life of Lao-tzu, teacher of Taoism in the fifth century BCE. The principal historical account of his life must be doubtful, because it was written around 400 years after his death. Some scholars have argued that he may be an entirely mythical figure.

One legend about Lao-tzu's birth emphasizes his great wisdom. It tells that Lao-tzu's mother was a virgin who carried him in her womb for no fewer than 80 years, and his father was a beam of sunlight. With such origins and after such a long gestation period, the philosopher, on the day of his birth, was as wise as an 80-year-old sage and had a full head of gray hair.

In adulthood, Lao-tzu occupied the position of diviner to the royal court of the Zhou dynasty, where he is reputed to have taught Confucius himself. Taoists like to say that Confucius was Lao-tzu's worst pupil; according to the Taoist scholar Zhuangzi (Chuang-tzu), when Confucius sought out Lao-tzu, determined to talk to him about humanity and duty, Lao-tzu reputedly said: "Seagulls do not become white by washing themselves every day; crows do not become black by dipping themselves daily in ink. In these cases, black and white are natural characteristics, so it cannot be said that one is better than the other. One who understands the Tao and employs humanity and duty to distinguish between good and evil is making the same mistake." Confucius was said to have been so impressed by Lao-tzu that he likened his teacher to a dragon riding the wind and clouds of the heavens.

This Chinese illustration from 1750 CE depicts Lao-tzu's departure from his native land on the back of a water buffalo.

According to other legends, as the Zhou dynasty began to decline, Lao-tzu became increasingly disenchanted with his own life and the general social conditions in China. One day, he decided that he could tolerate it no longer and rode off on a water buffalo to the far west. It is said that, shortly before leaving China, he wrote the *Tao Te Ching* (*Classic of the Way and Its Virtue*) and handed the manuscript to the guardian of the mountain pass through which he was traveling. He then took leave of China forever. Some say that he made his way to India, where he taught a modified version of his theories, which became known as Buddhism.

things to an end." The emphasis of the two philosophies is notably different; the Tao of Taoism is a metaphysical-individualistic concept, whereas the Tao of Confucianism offers the ideal of correct behavior in a social context.

Mencius

Subsequent philosophers expanded and developed the teachings of Confucius and Lao-tzu. The most important later Confucian thinker was Mengzi (Meng-tzu; c. 371–289 BCE), who is known in the West as Mencius, the Latin form of his name.

Mencius advocated humane government. In a time when rulers were believed to be granted their positions by the mandate of heaven, Mencius emphasized the duty of the ruler to the people and insisted that government be exercised on behalf of the people. He argued that subjects had the right to oppose and even depose an unjust ruler; if rebellion occurred against a king, it indicated that heaven had withdrawn the mandate by which the king was in power.

Mencius addressed Hui, the king of the state of Liang, in the following terms: "If you, oh king, do not interrupt the normal course of farming by putting the farmers under arms, then there should be a surplus of grain. If fine-meshed nets are not used for fishing, there should be plenty of fish and turtles. If trees are cut at the right time, then there should be an inexhaustible quantity of wood. If the entire supply of grain, fish, and wood is not used, the result will be that people can maintain the living and mourn the dead to their complete satisfaction. Maintenance

This dagger was made in China during the Zhou dynasty around 500 BCE. Its handle is made of gold encrusted with turquoise gemstones and glass.

of the living and mourning for the dead is the beginning of true kingship."

On another occasion, the king is reputed to have asked Mencius to identify what advantages—if any—that such practices would have for his country. Mencius replied: "But why must you speak of an advantage? It is always simply a question of humanity and doing your duty, that is all. When a king says, 'How can I benefit my country?' then the great people of the kingdom say, 'How can I benefit my family?' and the lower classes say, 'How can I benefit myself?' The state is imperiled when the classes fight with one another over benefits.... Let your Majesty speak only of humanity and of doing his duty."

The main contention made by Mencius was that people are inherently good. He illustrated this with the observation that if a person sees a child standing on the edge of a well where he or she is in danger of falling in and drowning, that person will surely rush over to rescue the child. He argued that it is only the circumstances in which people live that prevent their inherent goodness from constantly finding expression; since moral goodness is part of each person's nature, all human beings are equal and anyone can become a great sage. Mencius believed that this equality lay behind the people's right to overthrow a wicked government.

This 18th-century-CE portrait is of Mengzi (Meng-tzu), the influential later Confucian thinker known in the West as Mencius.

Legalism versus Confucianism

In time, Confucianism would exert a defining influence on political ideology, not only in China but throughout eastern Asia. In the short term, however, although the teachings of Confucius and Mencius were widely studied and discussed, the Confucians were largely marginalized. Few of Confucius's followers were able to obtain positions in government, and those who did acquire positions of power were frequently the objects of mild ridicule. Because many Confucian texts discussed the importance of correct ritual, Confucians were criticized for what was perceived as their excessive concern with trivial matters that were of no practical use to society. In the short term, the legalists had greater success.

Legalism was a rationalist philosophy of government. It originally developed from the teachings of Confucians such as Xunzi (Hsün-tzu; c. 298–230 BCE), who took issue with the theories of Mencius and argued that humans had evil in their nature and therefore required explicit controls to regulate their conduct. Under the Qin (Ch'in) dynasty that came to power in 221 BCE, the subordination of personal freedom to authority became the dominant philosophy. Two outstanding philosophers—Han Fei (Han-fei-tzu; d. 233 BCE) and Li Si (Li Ssu; c. 280–208 BCE)—expanded the arguments of Xunzi into the philosophy of legalism, laying their emphasis on the necessity of controlling the inherent sinfulness of humans and punishing wrong behavior.

THE THREE DOCTRINES

The philosophical religion of Buddhism was imported into China in the first century CE following Chinese contact with central Asia as a result of the silk trade. The three teachings of Confucianism, Taoism, and Buddhism then coexisted in China for several centuries and became known as the Three Doctrines. Few people adhered strictly to any one of these religions; most people mixed and matched elements of all three schools of thought in their religious practices.

Buddhism, which grew from the teachings of Siddharta Gautama (the Buddha; c. 563–483 BCE), was established in northeastern India by the fourth century BCE and came to China principally in the form of the Mahayana (Greater Vehicle) tradition that emerged in the first century CE. The Mahayana form of Buddhist thought viewed the historical Buddha as an incarnation of a transcendent Buddha and emphasized the importance of compassion. It argued that the supreme goal for a Buddhist was to become a bodhisattva, a person who had reached nirvana or enlightenment but chose to return to earth through reincarnation in order to help others toward the same goal.

In the third century CE, Confucianism underwent a complete reinterpretation based on the *I Ching* (*Classic of Changes*), one of the Five Classics of Chinese philosophy, and the *Tao Te Ching* (*Classic of the Way and Its Virtue*), a Taoist work attributed to Lao-tzu. Under the influence of those two books, Confucianism developed into a value system that codified and reflected the individual's desire for self-determination and personal salvation.

The Hanging Monastery in Shanxi (Shan-hsi) Province is one of the thousands of Buddhist structures in China.

According to the precepts of legalism, effective rule depended on the absolute authority of a ruler, his army, and his administrative apparatus; the people had to be kept in check by a rigidly applied system of punishments and rewards established through detailed legislation. Han Fei wrote: "We must not listen to those who argue on behalf of humanity and duty because, if they are heeded, nothing practical will any longer be achieved. Also, those who apply themselves to culture and scholarship must not be taken into the service because, if they are, they impede the application of the law."

The Qin rulers—who had declared themselves emperors—attempted to impose legalism at the expense of other programs of thought. In 213 BCE, legalism was declared China's state doctrine, and the emperor ordered the burning of all books other than histories, divination guides, and medical and agricultural textbooks. Totalitarian government did not last long; in 206 BCE, a rebel army officer named Liu Bang (Liu Pang) proclaimed the new Han dynasty.

The Han, who ruled until 220 CE, rejected legalism in 136 BCE and adopted Confucianism as their underlying philosophy of government. They combined Confucianism with ancient Chinese ideas of the cosmos. Rather than simply exercise power, rulers had to legitimize it by determining the will of heaven. The policy was a new manifestation of the old idea of the mandate of heaven, and indeed, the Han emperors became known as the sons of heaven. Heaven's approval or disapproval of imperial rule could be signaled by natural phenomena, such as storms and earthquakes, which were regarded as portents.

The Han emperors adopted the Confucian principles of equality for all and the appointment of officials on the basis of merit. They established written examinations for entrance to government service and required the study of Confucianism, establishing an official academy (based on the Five Classics) for public administrators.

秦李斯

This undated woodcut depicts Li Si (Li Ssu), a leading proponent of legalism in the third century BCE.

See also:

China's Imperial Dynasties (volume 7, page 894) • The Early History of China (volume 7, page 870)

CHINA'S IMPERIAL DYNASTIES

At the start of the Common Era, China was ruled by the Han dynasty. During this period, the country enjoyed considerable power and prosperity. The centuries following the Han dynasty's demise in 220 CE, however, saw the unity of China threatened.

By the end of the third century BCE, the Qin (Ch'in) dynasty had been fatally weakened by rebellions against excessive taxation. Its final collapse, in 206 BCE, was precipitated by an insubordinate army officer named Liu Bang (Liu Pang). At first just one of many rebel leaders, Liu Bang was popular with the masses, possibly because he shared their peasant origins. He soon became leader of the whole uprising. Having established a firm power base, he declared himself emperor, an act that marked the formal foundation of the Han dynasty. Liu Bang was also known as Gaozu (Kao-tsu).

By 202 BCE, Liu Bang had eliminated virtually all internal opposition to his rule, either by force of arms or by diplomacy. He reduced the tax burden on the peasants, who responded by working more efficiently, thereby reviving the rural economy. Liu Bang maintained China's traditional feudal structure and rewarded his allies and relatives with their own hereditary kingdoms.

The kingdoms did not maintain their independence for long. Subsequent Han rulers retook direct control of virtually all the lands in their domain, thereby establishing the dynasty's reputation for reform. The other major change implemented by the Han emperors was the introduction of Confucianism as an official ideology.

Han Confucianism

The Qin dynasty had set great store by the teachings of Xunzi (Hsün-tzu; c. 298–230 BCE), a philosopher who took the view that people were by nature evil and needed strict laws and punishments to regulate their conduct. Xunzi gave the Qin emperors a rationale for minimizing individual freedom and for exercising unlimited control over society.

Confucianism, in contrast, regarded the individual as the most important unit in the hierarchies of family, society, and state. Its founder, Confucius (551–479 BCE), developed his philosophy while advising the rulers of various states. He sought to re-establish social order through personal morality, a code of behavior learned by studying the rules of propriety outlined in the literature of the Shang dynasty (c. 1766–1050 BCE).

The Han emperors maintained the Qin dynasty's administrative apparatus but modified many of its policies to suit their own ends. When they formally adopted Confucianism in 136 BCE, they espoused the philosophy's principle of encouraging learning, on the basis that educated individuals are of greater use to society than unenlightened people.

The Han rulers made it compulsory for holders of public office to pass examinations. This development ensured that officials earned their positions based on

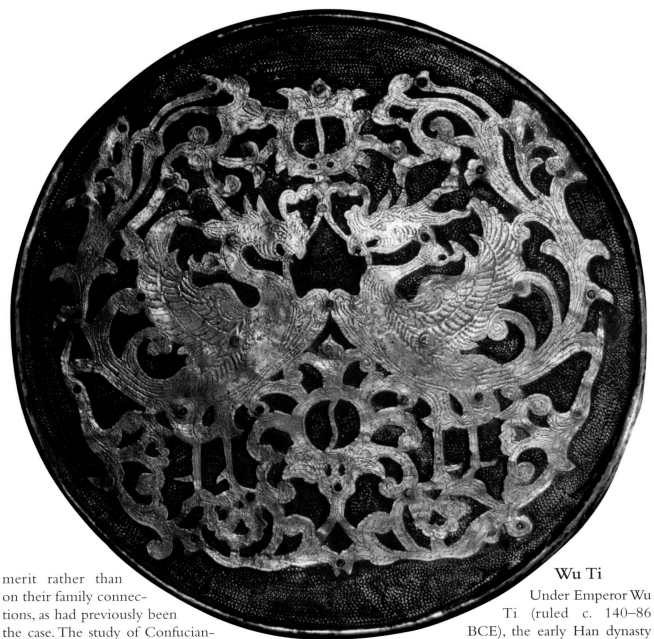

This back of a mirror, made during the Tang period (618–907 CE), depicts two phoenixes. The phoenix was the symbol of China's empress.

merit rather than on their family connections, as had previously been the case. The study of Confucianism became an essential requirement for government service, and a university for bureaucrats was set up in the late second century BCE. The emperors reorganized the system of taxation, generally reducing the financial burden on the populace and establishing uniform levies throughout the empire to replace excessively complex local laws and currencies. The Han rulers also encouraged people to maintain grain reserves as a precaution against famine.

Wu Ti

Under Emperor Wu Ti (ruled c. 140–86 BCE), the early Han dynasty reached its peak of expansion. In the west, Chinese forces advanced into the valley of the Jaxartes River (in present-day Kazakhstan), where they fought the Xiongnu (Hsiung-nu), an ancient people about whom little is known, other than that they may have been related to the Huns. Wu Ti's general, Zhang Qian (Chang Chien), then consolidated China's position by negotiation, forming alliances with Samarkand, Bactria, Bokhara, and Ferghana. (The remains of

This bronze plaque depicting a man riding a camel was made during the time of the Han dynasty (206 BCE–220 CE).

some of the forts and fortifications built to hold back the Huns may still be seen in the Gobi Desert.) China then took the offensive in the north and conquered the Tarim Basin. Wu Ti eventually established imperial control over the southern part of Manchuria and northern Korea. In the south, he conquered the island of Hainan. He established colonies in Annam and Korea and ultimately extended Han authority from Korea to Tonkin in Vietnam, although much of the area, especially south of the Yangtze River, was not completely assimilated.

These campaigns cost more money than the Chinese treasury had at its disposal. In an attempt to make up the shortfall, Wu Ti and his successors increased taxation and reintroduced government monopolies, which had been abolished in the early years of the Han dynasty.

Having overstretched itself in foreign adventures, the Han dynasty rapidly lost much of its authority. Its decline was hastened by a series of rulers who came to the imperial throne in infancy. Their mothers governed on their behalf and undermined the established meritocracy by appointing relatives to key government positions. The regencies created an atmosphere of intrigue and partisanship.

The financial situation deteriorated as provincial landholding families, having refused to pay taxes, were given tax-exempt status. The government still needed funds, so it passed the burden on to the peasants by increasing their indebtedness. For many farmers, working conditions became intolerable. They divided their landholdings among family, friends, and the highest bidders and looked for other means of support. Some former farmers turned to banditry; others took up arms against imperial rule.

The Xin dynasty

Wang Mang was the usurper who founded the short-lived Xin (Hsin) dynasty. His father's half sister was an empress of the Han dynasty. In 16 BCE, Wang Mang was given a noble title and later appointed to the regency. He outmaneuvered his opponents and had his own daughter enthroned as empress under a 14-year-old emperor who died suddenly and mysteriously the same year. Wang Mang was accused of murder by his enemies. He solved the succession problem by selecting from the possible claimants a 1-year-old boy who was not officially enthroned but called the Young

This 17th-century-CE Chinese painting depicts the emperor Wu Ti, who ruled during the early Han period.

Prince. Wang Mang then assumed the position of acting emperor.

Having subdued his opponents, Wang Mang announced that heaven was calling for an end to the Han dynasty and that he had the mandate to create a new one. On January 10, 9 CE, Wang Mang ascended the throne and proclaimed the foundation of the Xin dynasty.

Wang Mang maintained the agrarian and monetary policies of the Han dynasty. He supported scholarship and led China successfully in its foreign policy. He was an unscrupulous legal hardliner who had three of his own sons executed for breaking the law, along with a grandson and a nephew.

The Xin dynasty was cut short by a natural catastrophe. Between 2 and 5 CE, and again in 11 CE, the Yellow River changed its course, devastating a large populated area. Famine and epidemics led to mass migration and civil war. One of the rebellious peasant groups, known as the Red Eyebrows because they painted their faces to look like demons, defeated Wang Mang's armies. Other

THE SILK ROAD

The Silk Road was the earliest trade link between China and Europe and northern Africa. There is evidence that inhabitants of the Sahara Desert were importing goods overland from eastern Asia as early as 7500 BCE. The route became established as a caravan trail in the second half of the first millennium CE.

In China, the terminus of the Silk Road was in Chang'an (modern Xi'an). From there, the route stretched 5,000 miles (8,000 km) westward along the Great Wall of China, then divided into two parallel passages to the north and south of the Tibetan Plateau. The branches rejoined at Kokand (a city in modern Uzbekistan), then went on across Afghanistan and Mesopotamia to the Mediterranean Sea.

The main Chinese export was the silk that gave the trail its name. The eastbound trade was mainly gold, silver, and wool. Few people made the full journey from one end of the route to the other; most people handled the goods for no more than a few hundred miles.

This bronze statuette of a horse was made during the second century CE.

rebellions ensued. On October 4, 23 CE, the rebels broke into the capital. The imperial palace was set on fire. Together with around 1,000 of his supporters, Wang Mang made a last-ditch defense of his throne, but he was killed in the ensuing battle. The short-lived Xin dynasty came to an end on October 6.

The Second Han period

After the fall of the Xin dynasty, the Han returned to power. However, the problem of infant emperors and incompetent regent-mothers reemerged. The situation created administrative chaos that was in sharp contrast to the discipline and order of the early Han period. The emperors turned to the court eunuchs (castrated men) for support, but the latter demanded increased political power in return for their assistance. Factional struggles led first to intrigue and later to open conflict.

The later Han rulers also faced other problems. During the dynasty's earlier decline, many of the great landowners had achieved local autonomy and established their own private armies. In 184 CE, Taoist (Daoist) societies organized rebellions against imperial rule. The Yellow Turbans (a group named for the color of their headscarves) caused devastation in Shandong (Shantung) until 204 CE. In Sichuan (Szechwan), the Five Pecks of Rice Society (named for its annual subscription fee) continued its wars for a decade. The rebels were eventually halted in 215 CE by the Han general Cao Cao (Ts'ao Ts'ao). Five years later, the general's son took the imperial throne, thereby establishing the Wei dynasty.

Although the Han dynasty ended disastrously, it had been a period of major cultural and economic development. During the reign of Wu Ti, Sima Qian (Ssu-ma Ch'ien; c. 145–90 BCE) had written the *Shi-ji* (*Shi-chi*; *Records of the Grand Historian*), an important work that provided a template for subsequent generations of Chinese historians.

Even the largely decadent later phase of the Han dynasty had its high points. The Silk Road, the trade route that stretched overland to Europe, was made safe again after a period in which its use had become dangerous. Caravan traffic soon topped the levels that had been reached under Wu Ti. One measure of the route's success was the export of Chinese silk to a distant place known in China as Ta-tsi Tsin and known in the West as the Roman Empire. The Han dynasty also witnessed the invention of the water clock and the sundial. In 105 CE, rags and plant fiber were first used to make paper; the creation of this revolutionary writing material is traditionally credited to a court eunuch named Cai Lun (Ts'ai Lun).

The Six Dynasties period

In the years following the fall of the Han dynasty, China fragmented into a number of kingdoms. This era is called the Six Dynasties period. Two rivals to the Wei dynasty, both also related to the Han dynasty, were established. The Shu dynasty (221–263 CE) was based in southwestern China, while the Wu dynasty (222–280 CE) was located in the Yangtze River Valley to the southeast.

This silver incense burner is an example of the levels of craftsmanship achieved by China's metalworkers during the Tang dynasty (618–907 CE).

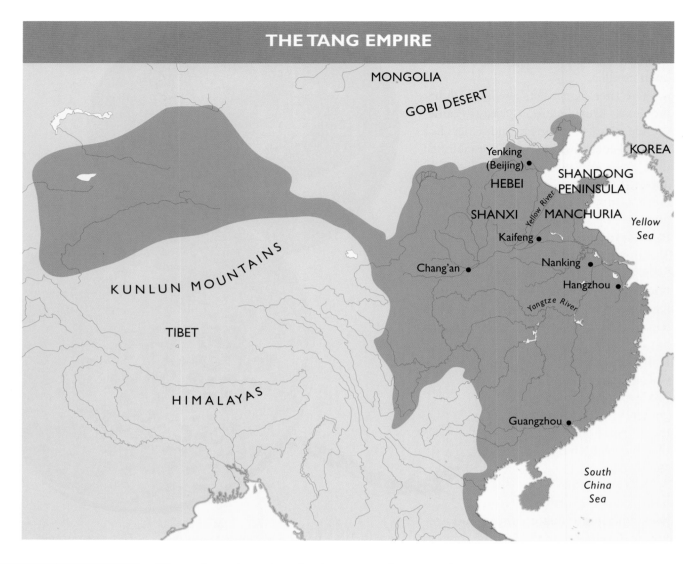

THE TANG EMPIRE

These three dynasties, also known as the Three Kingdoms, waged incessant and inconclusive warfare between 220 and 265 CE. In 265 CE, however, the Wei general Sima Yan (Ssu-ma Yen) seized the throne, establishing the Jin (Chin) dynasty (265–317 CE). By 280 CE, he had reunited north and south, and the dynasty remained stable until his death in 290 CE.

In 304 CE, non-Chinese tribes started to invade from the north. By 317 CE, they had wrested northern China from the Jin dynasty. They retained the conquered territories for almost three centuries, setting up 16 separate realms that were not accorded dynastic names. In the south, meanwhile, four Chinese dynasties ruled in turn.

The rest of Chinese society became feudal. Large landowners were able to run self-sufficient manors farmed by peasants who traded work for protection and became dependents of their lords. Most manors were well fortified and protected by private armies.

The Sui dynasty

In 581 CE, an army servant named Yang Jian (Yang Chien) seized the throne from the non-Chinese tribes in the north. He had himself proclaimed emperor, establishing the Sui dynasty, and proceeded to conquer southern China. After unifying

China, he centralized the administrative system established by the Han dynasty and revived the competitive examinations for bureaucrats (mandarins). He made Confucianism the state ideology but welcomed the contribution of Taoism (Daoism) and Buddhism.

During his short reign, Yang Jian accomplished a great deal. He ordered the construction of a canal—later part of the 1,000-mile (1,600-km) Grand Canal—to carry farm produce from the Yangtze River Delta to the northern area of the country. He repaired the Great Wall of China and built a series of splendid palaces and Buddhist temples in his new capital of Chang'an (present-day Xi'an). Yang Jian oversaw the overhaul of the country's administration and the modernization of its criminal law system. He reclaimed northern Vietnam, but his efforts in Manchuria and Korea were unsuccessful. In 618 CE, the Sui dynasty was overthrown by Li Yuan, who founded the Tang dynasty and took the name Gaozu (Kao-tsu).

The Tang dynasty

The Tang dynasty (618–907 CE) introduced significant and enduring government reforms, including a reorganization of the civil service that lasted into the 20th century CE. The emperor Gaozu rewrote the government entrance examination and founded the Han-li Academy for history. He centralized the administration and developed a new code of administrative and penal law. By the time Gaozu abdicated in 626 CE, China was the largest empire in the world. Its generals occupied parts of Turkestan, Korea, Pamir (part of present-day Tajikistan), and Tibet. After the conclusion of favorable treaties with the peoples of central Asia, China dominated the Tarim Basin. The influence of the Tang dynasty was also evident in Japan, southern Manchuria, and northern Vietnam.

This pair of silver scissors was made during the Tang dynasty (618–907 CE).

Foreign trade expanded along the overland caravan routes and across the seas through the port of Guangzhou (Canton). One great emperor followed another, and the country prospered as never before. Commercial success was reflected in a golden age of art and literature. In the early Tang era, the capital, Chang'an, was renowned for its culture and religious toleration. Buddhism reached its peak of popularity.

Although the power of the Tang dynasty began to decline in the eighth century CE, the empire's artistic output remained outstanding and prolific. More than 1,000 major poets are known from this period. Literature was made more accessible than ever before by the development of printing, which permitted large-scale production of texts; previously, written works could be reproduced only by manual transcription. The later Tang emperors published a newsletter for their officials throughout the country. The Tang dynasty also used the new invention to print the world's first paper money.

The peasants' tax liability was calculated on the basis of the amount of land they held. The flaw in the system was that it assessed indebtedness per capita; if a man divided his allotment among two or more heirs, each of them had to pay the same amount as their father had paid even though they had no more than half as much land. The problem was exacerbated by rapid population growth and by the resentment caused when some favored people were still granted tax-free status for their estates. Peasants who could not pay the taxes on their allotments ran away, thereby depriving the government of revenue

time, China became increasingly influenced by Taoism (Daoism), a philosophy, founded by the Chinese author Lao-tzu (Laozi; c. 570–490 BCE), that emphasized harmony with the Way (Tao; Dao) of nature and opposed government interference in individuals' affairs.

The tolerance shown by the early Tang dynasty toward Buddhism and Taoism gave way in the latter part of the era to a revival of Confucianism, particularly among the growing class of public officials. Buddhism came to be regarded as an attack on the social order, something that could not be condoned by the state. While Buddhism was, by this time, too firmly established to be rooted out completely, China's growing fear of the exotic led to the proscription of other foreign cultural traditions. Several Buddhist monasteries were forcibly dissolved, at great profit to the state treasuries.

The Song dynasty

After the last emperor of the Tang dynasty was deposed in 907 CE, China again experienced a period of internal strife. Five short-lived dynasties followed in sequence in the Yellow River Valley. A number of other kingdoms were established at around the same time, most of them in southern China. In the north, the Khitan Mongol Liao dynasty (907–1125 CE) expanded from Manchuria and Mongolia into parts of China—Hebei (Hopei) and Shanxi (Shan-hsi)—and made Yenking (modern Beijing) the southern capital of a Sino-Khitan empire.

China remained divided until 960 CE, when General Zhao Kuangyin (Chao K'uang-yin) seized the throne and declared himself the first emperor of the Song (Sung) dynasty (960–1279 CE). By 978 CE, he had reconquered nearly all of China apart from the areas held by the Khitan Mongol Liao dynasty. He made Kaifeng his capital.

This silver brooch, depicting a mythological animal, was made in China around 850 CE.

and depleting the army (all adult males were required to perform a period of military service). Eventually, the Chinese were forced to hire foreign mercenaries to serve in the border militia. In 751 CE, the soldiers of fortune were blamed for a defeat by the Arabs that cost the Tang dynasty the Tarim Basin.

Tang Buddhism and Taoism

Buddhism had spread to southern China from India and, by the fourth century CE, had become the religion of around one-half of the world's population. Much of northern China was then converted, and by 600 CE, most of the country was Buddhist. The spread of Buddhism was greatly aided by widespread disillusionment with Confucianism, which had became equated with the maintenance of the status quo and corrupt officials. Buddhism—with its emphasis on morality, detachment from earthly things, and inner tranquility—offered a welcome, untainted alternative. Around the same

The reimposition of order stimulated a revival of trade and general prosperity. Towns expanded, and with their growth came a host of new civic services and amenities: fire departments, municipal police, orphanages, hospitals, public baths, welfare agencies, and even an agricultural testing station. The Song emperors subordinated the army to the civil service and opened the entrance examination for the latter to applicants who were outside the nobility. Education, the arts and literature, philosophy, engineering, astronomy, and mathematics all flourished. Women were allowed to participate in these activities, and several females were among the preeminent poets and painters of the age.

The military, however, was weakened and suffered frequent defeats by the Liao. In 1004 CE, the Song rulers formally ceded the northern territories that were already occupied by the Liao and agreed to pay them an annual tribute. In 1044 CE, the Song were forced to make further yearly payments to the Xi Xia (Hsi Hsia), a Tangut tribe that lived on China's northwestern border.

Tributes were costly, as were military operations and the maintenance of the large bureaucracy. The economy was unable to keep up with the burgeoning population. There was bitter rivalry over various proposals for reform. To survive, the Song dynasty allied with the Jin (Chin) dynasty (1122–1234 CE) of northern Manchuria against the Liao. Together, they defeated the Liao in 1125 CE. However, the Jin then moved against the Song, seizing Kaifeng in 1126 CE.

The loss of Kaifeng marked the start of the Southern Song era. The Song retreated to Hangzhou and made the city their capital in 1135 CE. As its name

This bronze Chinese statuette from around 800 CE depicts a lokapala, a Buddhist deity who protected the dead.

suggests, the dynasty controlled only southern China, but its economic and artistic accomplishments outstripped those of the earlier Song dynasty. It showed little sign of any insurmountable problems when it was faced with a new threat, the Mongols.

The Mongols

Around 1200 CE, Genghis Khan led the first Mongol horsemen over the Great Wall of China, which marked the southern border of his father's tribal domain. Having inherited the leadership of a loose confederation of nomadic shepherding tribes, Genghis Khan had built an intensely loyal and disciplined fighting force that was characterized by superb horsemanship and archery, extraordinary mobility, and astonishing cruelty.

The Mongols had no desire to forge a lasting empire in China through systematic conquest; their objective was merely seasonal plunder. For years, the Mongol hordes (a horde was a unit of 10,000 soldiers) entered China in the summer to pillage and returned to the Mongolian steppes for the winter. Their marauding power had a devastating effect on morale in China. Many Chinese generals and high officials defected, providing the illiterate Mongols with the services of people who could read and write and who were familiar with technologies unknown to them.

In 1213 CE, Ghengis Khan led his armies to the Shandong Peninsula. In 1215 CE,

This black vase, made during the Song dynasty (960–1279 CE), was used to carry tea.

he razed Yenking (modern Beijing), extending his control over the Jin dynasty in northern China. Genghis Khan died in 1227 CE, but his grandsons, Mangu and Kublai Khan, eventually completed the conquest that he had started; they seized almost all of China.

Kublai Khan ultimately succeeded to the Mongol leadership in 1260 CE, establishing his capital, Khan-balik (Cambaluc, near modern Beijing), four years later. The city became an international center of great renown. Kublai Khan defeated the Southern Song dynasty in 1279 CE. The rest of China was already in Mongol hands, but the Chinese navy still tried to defend the empire. In the end, the navy suffered overwhelming defeat. The admiral of the fleet drowned, holding in his arms the infant who was the last of the Song emperors.

In the same year, Kublai Khan established the Yuan (Yüan) dynasty, becoming its first emperor. Although Kublai Khan was a committed Buddhist and made Buddhism the state religion, he permitted other forms of worship in his realm. He adopted the Chinese bureaucratic system but excluded Chinese people from positions of authority, replacing them with Mongols.

After Kublai Khan's death in 1294 CE, the Mongols chose his grandson as successor. The dynasty remained in power in spite of growing resentment at all levels of Chinese society; the forces of opposition were fatally weakened by conflicting objectives and a lack of common purpose. Chinese officials, primarily Confucians, objected to their reduced status; Chinese peasants, meanwhile, objected to new taxes.

This 14th-century-CE Persian manuscript illustration depicts the Mongol leader Genghis Khan fighting the Chinese.

The Ming dynasty

In the 14th century CE, crop failures, resultant famine, and inflation, together with devastating floods, intensified civil discontent. Provincial rebellions began to occur. By the 1360s CE, a former Buddhist monk named Zhu Yuanzhang (Chu Yüan-chang) had gained control of the Yangtze River Valley. After years of struggle against rival claimants, he finally declared himself emperor in 1368 CE, taking the title Hong-wu (Hung-wu). He became the first emperor of the Ming dynasty, which was to last until 1644 CE.

See also:

Early Chinese Thinkers (volume 7, page 882) • The Early History of China (volume 7, page 870) • The Mongols (volume 9, page 1218)

THE EMERGENCE OF JAPAN

Japan emerged as a political entity no later than the sixth century CE, around the same time that Buddhism arrived in the country. The next 1,000 years were characterized by periods of economic growth and political development interspersed with civil wars.

Until the end of the Pleistocene epoch, around 10,000 BCE, the 3,000 islands that make up present-day Japan were joined to mainland Asia. The earliest vestiges of human occupation—rudimentary tools and piles of mollusk shells discarded after the contents had been eaten—date from around 200,000 years ago. The first residents of Japan were hunter-gatherers who arrived from the Korean Peninsula across land that is now covered by the Korea and Tsushima straits and from northeastern Siberia across land that is now covered by the Soya and Tsugaru straits.

The Jomon period

At the end of the Pleistocene epoch, sea levels rose, and Japan took on its modern topographical form—an archipelago off the eastern coast of Asia. By around 7500 BCE, the inhabitants lived mainly by hunting and fishing, although there were still some gatherers who subsisted on nuts and roots. Agriculture developed around this time, as evidenced by the discovery of the remains of blunt axes that appear to have been used for digging soil rather than cutting. The two principal crops were vegetables: yams and taros.

The period's main artistic development was pottery with cordlike surface patterns known as jomon. The word was later adopted as the name for the whole culture. During the next 7,000 years, the decorations became increasingly artistic and ornate, and they developed notable regional variations. Among the other significant archaeological finds from the Jomon period are semisubterranean pit houses with thatched roofs supported by posts.

The Yayoi period

The Jomon period was succeeded around 250 BCE by the Yayoi period. The name is derived from the district of Tokyo in which the earliest artifacts of the period were discovered. Yayoi pottery was less elaborately decorated than Jomon pottery, but it was turned on wheels and fired at higher temperatures than its predecessor, indications that the products were primarily for use rather than for ornamentation.

The Yayoi period also saw the emergence of weaving (whereas Jomon clothing had been made principally of bark) and of metal containers that were used in the cultivation of rice. Rice-growing was new to the area and had probably been imported by refugees from China during the Period of the Warring States (c. 475–221 BCE).

This mask depicting a demon was made in the 13th century CE. It was originally worn by performers in No dramas.

JAPAN IN THE MIDDLE AGES

CHINA

HOKKAIDO

Sea of
Japan

JAPAN

HONSHU

Kamakura ●

● Heian-kyo (Kyoto)

● Heijo (Nara)

KOREA

Pacific Ocean

✗ Hakata Bay

KYUSHU

KEY

✗   Major battle

The unification of Japan

The Yayoi period lasted until the second or third century CE, when Japan entered the Iron Age. At some point between that time and 552 CE, the islands became united under an emperor. Exactly how and when that happened is unclear because there are no authoritative contemporary records. The earliest account of Jimmu, Japan's legendary first emperor, appears in *Kojiki* (*Records of Ancient Matters*), an oral-tradition epic that was not written down until 712 CE, at least a century and a half after the events it purports to describe. According to another early (but not necessarily reliable) source, the eighth-century-CE *Nihon shoki* (*Chronicles of Japan*), the nation was united by 369 CE, the year in which it dispatched troops to intervene in struggles on the Korean Peninsula.

In Japanese society, the role of the emperor was separated from that of the political power brokers. The ruler's main responsibility was to unite all the religious cults and philosophies that had proliferated regionally before unification. As part of the effort to achieve such unification, the emperor was worshipped as a descendant of the principal deity, Amaterasu, the sun goddess (see box, page 912). The emperor was also the head of the *uji* (clans) that practically ruled the country. The *uji* all had their own gods, but none were as powerful as Amaterasu. The imperial court was situated in the province of Yamato on the island of Honshu. That province gave its name to the next period of Japanese history.

The arrival of Buddhism

The emergence of Japan as a cohesive state during the Yamato period was aided and to a large extent implemented by the *be* or *tomo*, communities of workers who provided services to the emperor and the *uji* in times of peace and took up arms for them in times of war. The most

important lasting development under the Yamato was the introduction of Buddhism to Japan from Korea. The religion arrived in Japan around 550 CE. It is doubtful that there was any one, identifiable date for Buddhism's arrival; it is more likely that Buddhism was adopted

This vessel from around 5000 BCE displays the cord pattern that was distinctive of Jomon pottery.

BURIAL RITES

Much of the knowledge about the history of Japan before the Common Era is derived from archaeological excavations of tombs. The earliest human remains in Japan date from the Jomon period (c. 7500–250 BCE), during which bodies were buried in small pits, often in the fetal position, with knees tucked under the chin. Some bodies had their hands placed together on their chests and clasped stones, which are thought to have had some mystical significance; most of the pre-Buddhist religions in Japan were fertility cults.

Such burial practices were maintained by the Yayoi people, but by the third century CE, the Japanese had begun to bury their dead in large burial mounds, which were typically circular or keystone-shaped. For that reason, the Yamato period is alternatively known as the Tumulus (Tomb) period. The artifacts discovered in such earthworks demonstrate that, by that time, the Japanese attached great importance to weapons, which were often buried with their owners. Such tombs also contained hollow terra-cotta sculptures known as *haniwa*.

This undated illustration depicts Jimmu, the legendary first emperor of Japan.

establishment of Buddhism also inspired the first written works in the Japanese language. Buddhism soon developed a uniquely Japanese variant, known as Shintoism, that became the state religion. It retained that official status until the end of World War II in 1945 CE and still has millions of followers in spite of its disestablishment.

After a period of prosperity, the power of the Yamato court went into terminal decline toward the end of the sixth century CE as *uji* infighting weakened the court's authority. The clan that became dominant was the Soga, under Iname (ruled 536–570 CE) and his son Umako (ruled 570–626 CE). The Soga controlled the succession to the imperial throne but did not become emperors themselves; the title remained in a single family to preserve the unbroken line that could traditionally be traced back to Amaterasu. The Soga introduced a meritocratic system of rank in 603 CE and a comprehensive new code of government in 604 CE. The Soga were also keen promoters of Buddhism.

The Taika Reforms and *ritsuryo*

The Soga policies did not meet with universal approval, however, and in 645 CE, the Soga were driven into exile by opposition forces with Chinese aid. In 646 CE, the emperor Kotoku became the absolute ruler of Japan. He abolished private ownership of land and abolished the *be*, giving peasants their freedom and making them leaseholders of the state. These innovations—known as the Taika Reforms—led, in 702 CE, to the adoption of a state system closely modeled on that of China under the Tang dynasty (618–907 CE) but altered wherever necessary to suit local requirements. Under the new system—known as *ritsuryo*, a combination of the words *ritsu* (criminal code) and *ryo* (administrative and civil code)—the emperor was confirmed as

gradually over many years. Buddhist values became ingrained in Japanese life under Crown Prince Shotoku (ruled 593–622 CE), who also introduced the precepts of Confucianism and a constitution in which advancement was based more on merit than on heredity. The

the absolute ruler and high priest. In practice, however, Japan was governed by two authorities: the Dajokan (the council of state) and the Jingikan (the office responsible for divining the will of the gods).

In a further attempt to provide a counterbalance to the traditional Japanese practice of filling high positions with people of noble birth, the new system introduced a civil service examination that made it possible for ordinary people to gain appointment to government posts based on merit. Before long, however, the college that had been set up to train new candidates fell into disuse. The top jobs again became the exclusive property of noble families.

The *ritsuryo* system recognized two main classes of common people: freemen and slaves. Some freemen were engaged in manufacturing industries (smiths and tanners, for example), but most were farmers. In addition to their normal work (mainly in the paddy fields), the farmers were required to perform military service and as many as 60 days a year of labor on public works. They also had to bear the cost of transporting their produce to the capital. For freemen in the farthest outlying provinces, this financial burden was too much to bear, and when they defaulted and fled from their land, the central government was powerless to arrest them. In their absence, the state suffered serious losses of revenue.

The slaves belonged to the government, the nobles, and the priests and were supposed to provide their various masters with any service that was demanded. The slaves made up roughly one-tenth of the population.

Before long, it became apparent that Japan was not producing enough food to feed itself. The government responded to the crisis by relaxing its former stipulation that all land was the property of the state and allowing the private ownership of fields used for growing crops. That decision proved to be the death knell of the *ritsuryo* system.

Two capitals

In 710 CE, Heijo became Japan's first fixed capital; for many years previously, the capital had moved around with the emperor. The design of Heijo was based on the contemporary Chinese capital, Chang'an (modern Xi'an). Heijo did not retain

This giant statue of the Buddha, 11.5 m (38 feet) tall, is located at Kamakura.

its status for long; in 794 CE, the emperor Kammu (ruled 781–806 CE) transferred the capital to Heian-kyo (present-day Kyoto). In the meantime, the administration's search for new, arable land had taken the Honshu-based government into a war with Ezo (the northern part of Japan, roughly coextensive with the island of Hokkaido). For a time, the conflict was so intense that a military draft was introduced; one in three males between the ages of 20 and 60 had to serve in the army for four years.

The Fujiwara period

From the 9th century to the 12th century CE, the Japanese aristocracy was headed by the Fujiwara family. The Fujiwaras rose to prominence after the Taika

This haniwa horse was made around the sixth century CE. Haniwa were terra-cotta sculptures that were placed in graves.

JAPANESE GOD OF GODS

Amaterasu—the deity from whom the Japanese royal family claims descent—was born from the left eye of her father, Izanagi, who put her in charge of Takamagahara (the High Celestial Plain), the abode of all the other deities. Amaterasu ruled happily for a time but then withdrew to a cave after arguing with Susanoo, her brother. In her absence, the world was plunged into darkness. The other gods and goddesses eventually lured her out of hiding by telling her that another deity had taken her place.

In modern Japan, Amaterasu is worshipped mainly at the Grand Shrine in the city of Ise, where she is symbolized by a mirror that is one of the imperial treasures.

Reforms and put an end to interference in affairs of state by the network of provincial temples, monasteries, and nunneries established by the emperor Shomu (ruled 715–756 CE), who had been keen to entrench Buddhist values throughout Japan. The Fujiwara family later married into the imperial family and acted as the emperors' regents. The power of the Fujiwaras peaked in 858 CE, when the head of the family put his own seven-year-old grandson on the imperial throne.

The Fujiwara period witnessed a great flowering of literature. The earliest great work was *Kokin-shu* (905 CE), a collection of more than 1,000 poems. At the head of the renaissance were female authors, who tended to write in informal Japanese, rather than the stilted version of Chinese that was then the traditional form in Japan. The two greatest works of

the period are *Genji monogatari* (*The Tale of Genji*; c. 1010 CE), a work by Murasaki Shikibu, a minor noblewoman, and *Makura-no-soshi* (*The Pillow Book*; c. 1000 CE), a collection of scenes of court life by Sei Shonagon, a lady-in-waiting. *The Tale of Genji* is often described as the world's first novel. It relates the romantic escapades of the courtier of the title.

By the end of the 11th century CE, much of the land and property that had come into state hands at the time of the Taika Reforms had reverted to private ownership. As a result, the government lost valuable tax revenues and, consequently, much of its power and authority. Go-Sanjo (ruled 1060–1073 CE) was the first emperor in more than a century not to be related to the Fujiwaras. He tried to confiscate large estates without

Fujiwara authority and, although his attempt to stop the decline of the state was ultimately a failure, the end of an era was in sight; by 1110 CE, the Fujiwaras had been ousted.

The rise of the samurai

While the Fujiwaras had lived lavishly and paid little heed to what was going on around them, a new power had emerged in the land—the samurai, warriors who gradually took up key positions in provincial government and acquired extensive landholdings of their own. They raised private armies that grew unchecked and eventually became strong enough to challenge the central authorities. When it served their greater purpose, the samurai acted on behalf of the ruling classes. For example, in the

This manuscript illustration, created between the 12th century and the 14th century CE, depicts a battle during the Heiji Disturbance, a struggle that took place in 1159 CE between two groups of samurai.

11th century CE, they helped imperial forces to quell a rebellion in northeastern Japan. Eventually, the Minamoto and the Taira clans (the two leading bands of samurai) confronted each other in the Heiji Disturbance of 1159 CE. The Taira clan won the confrontation easily and became the major power in the land for a generation. However, in 1185 CE the tables were turned, and Minamoto Yoritomo set up a new government in the city of Kamakura. In 1192 CE, Yoritomo was named shogun (chief mil-

itary commander). It proved to be a pivotal moment in the history of Japan; the country would be ruled by the samurai until the restoration of imperial power in 1868 CE.

The military regime in Kamakura did not replace the civil administration in Kyoto, but the shogunate dominated Japanese affairs and appointed its own vassals. After the death of Yoritomo in 1199 CE, effective power passed to his widow's family, the Hojo clan. Not long afterward, however, a train of events

THE JAPANESE LANGUAGE

The Japanese language has no known relatives. Some researchers have tried to link it to the Altaic languages of northern and central Asia, such as Korean, Mongolian, and Manchu. However, those attempts have not been entirely convincing. Japanese has all the hallmarks of aboriginality; it is a language spoken by the inhabitants of a remote island that, until comparatively recently, experienced little outside influence.

Before the modern age, the only foreign country to have any significant effect on Japan was China. Since the earliest times, Japanese has been written with characters borrowed from the script of its mainland neighbor. The oldest written records in Japanese consist of a few names that appear in inscriptions from the late fifth century CE. The earliest substantial Japanese literary texts date from the eighth century CE, although they are known to have been based in part on older texts that have not survived. The language of these works is called Old Japanese.

Phonetic signs were later added to this early script by altering and simplifying a few of the borrowed Chinese characters. Chinese loan words proliferated; even today, more than half the words in Japanese are thought to be of Chinese origin. However, Japanese literary styles and genres have always remained distinct. There are many possible reasons for this, but one of the most important is that Japanese intellectuals often wrote in Chinese as well as in their native tongue, thus maintaining the separate nature of the two languages.

Middle Japanese is the name given to the language that was used in Japan between the late 11th century and the early 17th century CE. During this period, Japanese grammar and vocabulary made their big transition between Old Japanese and the language that is used today.

Old Japanese differs from Middle Japanese and modern Japanese in many ways. Its sound system, for example, had eight different vowels, while the modern language has only five. Old Japanese, however, lacked the contrast between long and short vowels that is so important in the modern language.

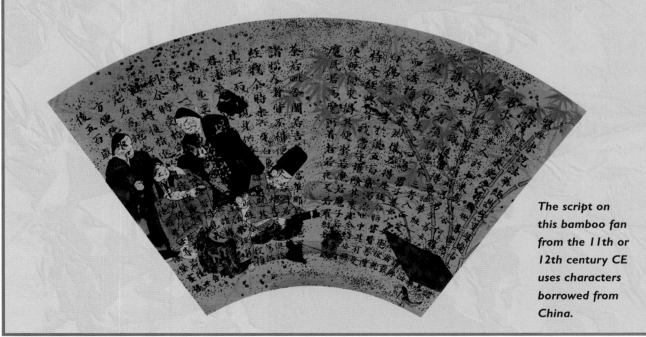

The script on this bamboo fan from the 11th or 12th century CE uses characters borrowed from China.

began that would arrest the development of Japan but help to establish the Japanese concept of nationhood.

The coming of the Mongols

In the first 50 years of the 13th century CE, the Mongols under Ghengis Khan carved out an empire that extended from the Pacific coast of Asia in the east to Poland in the west. Still seeking new worlds to conquer, the Mongols then turned their attention to Japan. In 1274 CE, an army of Mongols landed in Kyushu and advanced to Chikuzen; at the same time, another Mongol force came ashore in Hakata Bay. The Japanese

Minamoto Yoritomo became shogun (chief military commander) of Japan in 1192 CE. This Japanese painting was created around 1900 CE.

were ill prepared for such an onslaught, but a typhoon suddenly hit the coast and destroyed most of the invasion force; the survivors withdrew to Korea.

In 1281 CE, the Mongols came again. This time, the Japanese were expecting an invasion and had built defensive walls along their most threatened coasts, but they were still shocked by the size of the force. Again, the attackers brought two armies, one of 40,000 men and one of 100,000 men. The Mongols won the first engagement, at Hakata Bay, and it seemed as if their advance would be unstoppable. Just then, however, another typhoon intervened, destroying the invaders' ships at anchor and forcing their armies to break up in disarray. When the storm abated, the Japanese dealt harshly with the Mongols, reportedly killing four-fifths of them. Even then, the Mongols prepared another attack but abandoned the plans when their leader, Kublai Khan (Ghengis Khan's grandson), died in 1294 CE.

The successful defense of their land gave the Japanese a greater sense of common purpose than they had ever had before. They were also convinced that the intervention of the *kamikaze* (divine wind) on their behalf demonstrated that they were a special race, favored particularly by God.

Further civil strife

The Japanese may have succeeded in repelling the Mongol invaders, but the country had ruined itself financially in the process. To make matters worse, the feudal lords were very powerful, and their loyalty to the imperial throne was minimal. When Go-Daigo became emperor in 1318 CE and tried to get rid of the shoguns, he was exiled. He raised an army and regained power in 1333 CE, but he failed to reward adequately his main helper, Takauji of the Ashikaga family. Takauji retaliated by setting up a rival

emperor, and for almost 60 years, there were two imperial Japanese courts, one at Kyoto and the other at Nara.

Japan was reunited in 1392 CE, with the capital being in Kyoto. The early years of the 15th century CE saw the rise of a merchant class that grew rich through increased trade with China and Korea. However, Japan's economic growth suffered a damaging setback when a dispute over the succession to the shogunate led to the Onin War (1467–1477 CE). During and after this civil conflict, the Ashikagas lost all real power, although they remained nominally in control. In the absence of strong central government, the various lords of Japan—now mainly powerful landowners known as *daimyo*—vied for supremacy. As a result, the Onin War was merely a precursor to a much longer period of conflict, known as the Sengoku period. This time is also known as the Period of the Warring States, after its earlier Chinese equivalent.

Toward the end of the Sengoku period, in the 1540s CE, the first European explorers landed in Japan and introduced the natives to the art of musket construction, which revolutionized warfare on the islands. In 1549 CE, Francis Xavier (1506–1552 CE) became the first Jesuit missionary to set about establishing Catholicism in Japan. The spread of Christianity was encouraged by the rulers of Japan, because they were anxious to develop trading relations with Portugal, which soon became one of Japan's most important trading partners. The earliest Western accounts of Japanese society describe a complicated patchwork of independent domains (each legitimized by the payment of lip service to the imperial throne) that were gradually consolidating through commercial and military alliances.

See also:

China's Imperial Dynasties (volume 7, page 894) • The Mongols (volume 9, page 1218)

The Mongol fleet that attacked Japan in the 13th century CE is destroyed by a typhoon in this 19th-century-CE illustration.

INDIA'S FIRST CIVILIZATIONS

The earliest civilization in India emerged in the Indus River Valley in the third millennium BCE. Around 1,000 years later, Magadha emerged as the most important regional power. Magadha remained dominant until the start of the Common Era.

The first civilization of southern Asia emerged in the Indus River Valley around 2600 BCE. It resembled the civilization of Mesopotamia, arising on the arid flood plain of a great and unpredictable river where the need for large-scale irrigation and flood defense schemes led to the development of a well-organized hierarchical society.

The Indus Valley civilization

The first farming communities in southern Asia had developed at sites such as Mehrgarh in the mountains of Baluchistan as early as 6000 BCE and spread from there into the Indus Valley in the fourth millennium BCE. There was considerable interaction between the settlements in the valley and those in the highlands. Highland peoples took their flocks to winter in the valley and traded metals, semiprecious stones, and timber for grain and other foodstuffs. The early farming communities of the Indus Valley showed no signs of social ranking, but the transition to a hierarchical society occurred very rapidly around 2600 BCE. The change may have been a result of the establishment of trading contacts with Mesopotamia. Towns grew up in the Indus Valley as a result of this trade. The metals and other products from the highlands were consolidated in the towns and sent on to Mesopotamia. The growth

of trade also led to the development of several small towns, such as Nindowari, in the highlands.

Most of the cities and towns in the Indus Valley were small, but two, Mohenjo-Daro and Harappa (from which the Indus Valley civilization gets its alternative name, Harappan), had populations of 30,000–40,000 people, placing them among the largest Bronze Age cities anywhere. Both Mohenjo-Daro and Harappa, as well as several smaller cities such as Kalibangan, had mud-brick city walls, a citadel with public buildings and granaries, and streets laid out on a grid pattern.

Harappa and Mohenjo-Daro were first excavated in the early 20th century CE. Each city was 2–2.5 miles (3–4 km) in circumference. They both had superbly engineered water supplies and sewer systems with brick conduits. The citadel of each city was sited on raised ground on the western side. At Mohenjo-Daro, the streets, which ran north to south and east to west, were lined with two- and three-room dwellings, some of which were two or more stories tall and many of which had bathrooms and toilets. The houses

The city of Mohenjo-Daro is one of the most important archaeological remnants of the Indus Valley civilization.

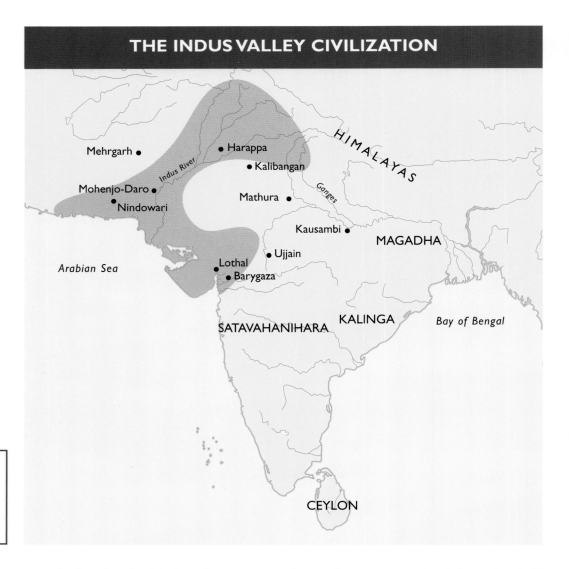

THE INDUS VALLEY CIVILIZATION

Mehrgarh •

• Harappa
• Kalibangan

Mohenjo-Daro •
• Nindowari

HIMALAYAS

Mathura •

Ganges

Kausambi •

MAGADHA

• Ujjain

Arabian Sea

• Lothal
• Barygaza

SATAVAHANIHARA

KALINGA

Bay of Bengal

CEYLON

KEY

Extent of the
Indus Valley
civilization

were built with fired bricks (in contrast to the sun-dried mud bricks used in Mesopotamia), and the walls were plastered with mud. Within the citadel at Mohenjo-Daro, archaeologists also discovered two assembly halls and a large communal bath lined with bitumen and surrounded by a veranda; the bath was probably used for ritual washing.

The civilization was literate, but its pictographic script has not been deciphered. As a result, the identity of the Indus people is unknown; they may have been related to the modern Dravidian peoples of southern India.

The people of the Indus Valley civilization traded with Mesopotamia and Egypt from a port at Lothal on the Gulf of Cambray, some 400 miles (650 km) south of Mohenjo-Daro. Indus craftsmen worked in wood, ivory, copper, and bronze, and they were the first people in history to make cotton cloth. The discovery of soapstone seals marked with carvings suggests that the Indus people may have worshipped the bull and a seated, horned god believed by many scholars to be the original of the Hindu deity Shiva. They also made terracotta figures of women thought to have been worshipped as fertility goddesses.

Harappa and Mohenjo-Daro were apparently built according to a predetermined plan, and it has been suggested

that there may be further settlements of the same culture still undiscovered beneath the sands of the Indus Valley. At its height, the Indus Valley civilization extended as far west as what is now the Pakistan–Iran border, as far north as the foothills of the Himalayas, and as far east as the land between the Ganges and Jumna rivers. After thriving for around 600 years, the Indus Valley civilization declined. The probable cause of the decline was a reduction in the trade that had made the region rich. The Indus Valley civilization may also have been disrupted by climatic and geological changes that led to rising sea levels and possibly an alteration in the course of the Indus River and the drying up of the

A water well stands among the ruined foundations of the city of Harappa in the Indus Valley.

The Indus River winds through Ladakh, a province in the Indian state of Jammu and Kashmir.

THE UNTOUCHABLES

Below the rungs of the caste ladder, outside the system of socially acceptable people, emerged a subcaste (which was millions strong) of people known as dalits (untouchables). Originally members of the lowest caste of shudras, the untouchables became a distinct grouping as the number of social strata increased.

The untouchables were assigned work that was regarded as unclean, such as killing animals, handling and processing animal carcasses, and clearing animal and human feces. Untouchables were not allowed to walk where the caste Hindus did or to use the same wells or temples. In the 20th century CE, Indian leader Mohandas Gandhi tried to end discrimination against the untouchables, declaring that they were Harijan (Children of God). He reinforced his point by setting an example and personally undertaking many of the tasks that were assigned to them.

The caste system in India was officially abolished in the middle of the 20th century CE by the country's first independent postcolonial government under Jawaharlal Nehru. Nevertheless, castes persisted as a social phenomenon, particularly in determining opportunities available to members of different classes.

Sarasvati-Ghaggar river system. At Mohenjo-Daro, archaeologists found the remains of unburied corpses in the city and evidence of damage by fire, suggesting that disease, natural disaster, or an attack by raiders may have precipitated the city's final collapse.

Whatever the cause, by around 1800 BCE, the Indus Valley cities were in decline, and a century later, they had been abandoned. Writing fell out of use. Life in the countryside continued unchanged for several centuries, suggesting that the civilization did not fall as a result of outside invasion. Around 1500 BCE, the Aryans, a seminomadic Indo-European pastoralist people, migrated into the Indian subcontinent from central Asia and occupied the northern half of the territory once covered by the Indus Valley civilization. Some aspects of Indus culture were absorbed by

This seal from around 2000 BCE depicts Pashupati, a horned deity that may be the Indus precursor of Shiva.

the Aryans. The pottery styles of the late Indus Banas culture survived and spread across most of southern India, but all remnants of the civilization itself were lost and not rediscovered until the 20th century CE.

Caste system

Even in decline, the culture of the indigenous inhabitants of northwestern India may have been superior to that of the Aryan incomers. It certainly presented a settled and urbanized way of life in contrast to that of the nomad-farmers. The invaders had significant military power, with their war chariots, and were well organized for conquest. However, it is not known whether they conquered the native descendants of the Indus Valley culture or merely settled among them and gradually came to dominate them. The attitude adopted by the newcomers seems to indicate that they were afraid of being overwhelmed by the native population. Dealing with a huge number of people spread over a vast area, the Aryans used separation and segregation as the means of preserving their own identity and of maintaining authority.

The result was the caste system. Probably instituted by the Aryans after their invasion, this system divided society into segregated groups based on birth and occupation. The word *caste*, however, came

This female terra-cotta figurine from the Indus Valley culture (third millennium BCE) was found at Mohenjo-Daro. It is 9 inches (23 cm) tall.

much later; it derives from the Portuguese word *casta* (breed) and was not introduced until the 16th century CE. The Aryans themselves used the term *varna* (the Sanskrit word for "color"), which suggests that the system may have had a racial origin, perhaps as a method of distinguishing the relatively light-skinned Aryan invaders from the darker natives.

When the Aryans first came to India, they were divided into three social groups: the warrior aristocracy, the priests, and the common people. There was apparently no consciousness of caste; professions were not hereditary, and there were no rules limiting social interaction among classes. The first step toward stratification—the institution of a strictly hierarchical caste system—came when the incomers began to view the indigenous peoples as being inferior, perhaps through nervousness that assimilation would lead to a loss of Aryan identity. The establishment of caste was also promoted by the specialization of labor that accompanied the transition from a nomadic, pastoral way of life to a settled agrarian economy. The Aryans used natives to trade their products, to manufacture tools and ornaments, to herd their flocks, to work their land, and to remove human and animal waste from their settlements. Each of these occupations became the basis of a different caste.

Initially, the Aryan social structure divided people into four main groups: the brahmins (priests), the kshatriyas (warrior aristocrats and kings), the vaishyas (farmers and traders), and the shudras (laborers, craftsmen, and servants). The shudras were principally the dark-skinned natives of the Indus Valley, added as a bottom tier beneath the three main groups of the incomers' society. In the hymns of the Aryans' scripture, the *Rig Veda*, the system was given a divine origin. The hymns described the creation of the universe—the sky, the moon, the sun, the earth, the air, the animals and birds, as well as the gods and wise men—from the parts of a primeval man named Purusha. The hymns also identified how the four classes of ancient India also emanated from Purusha: the brahmins were his mouth, the kshatriyas were his strong arms, the vaishyas were his powerful thighs, and the shudras were his feet.

By around 1000 BCE, the caste system had developed the basic social structure that survived until the mid-20th century CE. There were many castes (eventually more than 3,000) and very complex rules, with detailed taboos (prohibitions) regulating marriage, burial, and daily life—especially the preparation and sharing of food. Violation of the rules was thought to lead to ritual impurity; contact with a member of a lower caste was said to defile a person. People were forbidden to accept food cooked by a member of a lower caste because food that had been handled by the latter was considered unclean. Some people were believed to defile others merely by casting a shadow on them or by coming within a certain distance of them. There were various complicated procedures for ritual purification.

As the caste system developed, the divisions between each stratum of society tended to increase. Shudras became isolated; other castes were required to avoid them because contact was said to cause impurity. Shudras were excluded from religious ceremonies; no brahmin was permitted to accept a drink of water from a shudra, although he could accept a gift. There were even rules specifying the correct form of interaction between castes. According to the scripture called

Officially, the caste system in India has been abolished, but it retains some of its social power in rural areas of the country. These children are dalits (formerly untouchables) in the southern state of Tamil Nadu.

This terra-cotta grayware bowl is in the style that emerged on the Gangetic Plain between around 1000 and 800 BCE.

LEARNING IN ANCIENT INDIA

The Aryans believed that the universe was built on *rita* (order) and were inspired by this conviction to investigate natural forms and laws. They made astonishing breakthroughs in mathematics and medicine.

The familiar digits 1, 2, 3, and so on were first developed in India around 400 BCE. (They are known in English as "Arabic numerals" because they first came into use in Europe via the writings of Arab mathematicians who had learned the use of the numbers from India.) By the start of the Common Era, Indian mathematicians were using advanced concepts such as zero, decimal places, and even algebra. The Aryans also made significant advances in geometry.

Aryans believed that their sacrificial rituals had to be performed exactly as dictated by tradition, using precisely the right words and on altars in a fire pit of the right dimensions. Priestly manuals called *Sulbasutras* (dating from around 800 BCE and attached to the Vedas)

gave detailed instructions on the building of the altars and fire pits. The *Sulbasutras* show advanced knowledge of geometry and contain versions of the Pythagorean theorem (the formula, later attributed to the sixth-century-BCE Greek mathematician Pythagoras, for calculating the length of the longest side of a right-angled triangle using the lengths of the other two sides) and a number of accurate values for π (the ratio of a circle's circumference to its diameter).

Doctors in India developed the medical system of Ayurveda (life knowledge), which is still in use in the 21st century CE. Ayurveda used only herbal and other natural remedies and had eight principal areas: within the body; ear, nose, and throat; mothers, birth, and babies; pediatrics; infertility; toxicology (the study of poisons); mental illness; and surgery. As early as the eighth century BCE, doctors in India could perform cataract surgery and even plastic surgery (for example, to rebuild a damaged nose).

the *Atharva Veda*, a brahmin receiving a gift from a shudra must accept it in silence, while he should accept a gift from another brahmin with holy words, a gift from a kshatriya with thanks spoken aloud, and a gift from a vaishya with thanks murmured under his breath.

The Gangetic civilization

For five centuries, the seminomadic Aryans left little physical trace of their presence, but a mythic record of their migrations and wars with the indigenous

This Mauryan stone sculpture from the second century BCE depicts a creation goddess.

peoples has been preserved in the Vedic Hymns, the holiest books of the Hindu religion, which were transmitted orally for centuries until they were written down in the sixth century BCE. Around 1100 BCE, the Aryans adopted iron-working, possibly without outside influence, and soon afterward moved east to settle as rice farmers in villages on the plains of the Ganges River. The appearance on the Gangetic Plain, around 1000–800 BCE, of painted grayware pottery has been linked to Aryan settlement in the area. By 900 BCE, small tribal kingdoms and aristocratic tribal republics, known collectively as *janapadas*, were developing across the Gangetic Plain. By 700 BCE, they had coalesced into 16 *mahajanapadas* (great realms). By around 500 BCE, Magadha, under King Bimbisara, had emerged as the most powerful *janapada*. Hand in hand with the process of state formation came the growth of cities, many of which, including Ujjain and Kausambi, had mud-brick defensive walls. Around the same time, there were great developments in religion; it was the formative period of Hinduism, and the late sixth century BCE witnessed the lives and teachings of Mahavira, the founder of Jainism, and of Siddhartha Gautama, the Buddha himself.

By 500 BCE, the Gangetic civilization extended as far south as the Godavari River. Still farther south, there were iron-using, tribally organized farming peoples, many of whom buried their dead in megalithic cists (box-shaped tombs). Only toward the end of the first millennium BCE did state formation and urban development start in this area.

Mauryan India

In 500 BCE, northern India was divided into several Hindu kingdoms, the most powerful of which was Magadha, ruled by King Bimbisara. Southern India was

This stone relief effigy from the 11th century BCE depicts Agni, the Hindu god of fire.

still dominated by tribal peoples under Hindu influence. In 364 BCE, Magadha came under the control of the expansionist Nanda dynasty, which dominated northern India by around 340 BCE. The Nandas' reputation for oppressive taxation, however, led to their overthrow in a coup d'état by Chandragupta Maurya (ruled c. 321–293 BCE). Chandragupta's origins are obscure, but he appears to have been a military commander in the northwestern border provinces at the time of Alexander the Great's invasion of the Indus Valley. He fought against Greek outposts in the area and may have met Alexander.

By 311 BCE, Chandragupta had extended his kingdom to the Indus River, an advance that brought him into conflict with Seleucos, who had seized power after Alexander's death. In 305 BCE, Chandragupta defeated Seleucos and was ceded control of the whole Indus Valley in return for 500 war elephants. Chandragupta maintained a large standing army and imposed a harsh penal code on his people. He also created an effective central bureaucracy, which controlled economic activity and carried out road building, irrigation, and other public works. Around 293 BCE, Chandragupta abdicated in favor of his son, Bindusara (ruled c. 293–268 BCE), and became a Jain monk, dying around 286 BCE. Bindusara maintained his father's expansionist program and extended the Mauryan Empire far into southern India. In 268 BCE, he was succeeded by his son Ashoka (see box, page 930), one of India's most remarkable rulers. Reportedly overcome with remorse after a bloody conquest of the eastern coastal district of Kalinga in 261 BCE, Ashoka converted to Buddhism around 260 BCE.

Buddhism had its origins in the teachings of Siddharta Gautama, the Buddha (c. 563–483 BCE), in the heartland of Magadha. Buddhism began as just one of many sects influenced by, but reacting against, India's traditions of Brahmanic Hinduism. The missionary work started by Ashoka in 258 BCE began its transformation from minor sect to major world religion. Ashoka adopted the Buddhist principles of right conduct and nonviolence, assured neighboring states of his goodwill, ameliorated his grandfather's penal code, and sought to rule as far as possible by moral authority alone. To spread Buddhist values, he had edicts on morality and compassion carved on rock faces and pillars throughout his empire. More than 30 of these inscriptions survive, forming the most important source of information about Ashoka's reign. Ashoka intervened in doctrinal matters, and it was his initiative that led to the defining of the Buddhist canon at the Third Buddhist Council at Pataliputra around 240 BCE. Ashoka also promoted Buddhism abroad, sending missions to Indonesia, southern India, Ceylon, the Greek states of western Asia, and the nomads of central Asia.

Although Ashoka's empire was the largest state to exist in India before the coming of the Mughals in the 17th century CE, it did not long survive the ruler's death in 233 BCE. Much of Ashoka's empire was held only loosely, and the south was lost almost at once. By 200 BCE, the Bactrian Greeks had conquered the Indus Valley and restored Alexander's frontier in India. In the 180s BCE, the Bactrians briefly extended their control as far south as Barygaza and as far east as Mathura. The last Mauryan king was overthrown in 185 BCE by Pushyamitra Shunga, one of his generals.

This is one of the pillars erected during the reign of Ashoka and inscribed with holy Buddhist tales and precepts.

Under the Shunga dynasty, Magadha remained a major power, but after the dynasty fell in 73 BCE, the kingdom's power collapsed completely, and it became just one minor state among many on the Gangetic Plain. By that time, power had shifted to the northwest, where the Sakas, nomadic invaders from central Asia, had established a powerful kingdom around 94 BCE. By the beginning of the Common Era, the Saka kingdom was in decline, but around the year 50 CE, a second wave of nomads, the Kushans, invaded and founded another major kingdom in the northwest.

The advent of the Mauryan Empire accelerated state formation in southern India; trade contacts, colonies of northerners, and Buddhist missions ended the area's relative isolation. The first considerable state in the region, Kalinga, dominated eastern India and extended its power into the Gangetic Plain in the middle of the first century BCE under King Kharavela. Soon after Kharavela's death, however, Kalinga sank back into obscurity. More stable was the state of Satavahanihara, which also rose to prominence in the first century BCE and remained the dominant power in the south until the third century CE. Ceylon (modern Sri Lanka) was colonized around 500 BCE by Sinhalese people from southern India, and the native Veddas were pushed into the interior of the island. Traditionally, the first state in Ceylon was founded around 483 BCE, by King Vijaya in the north of the island. Ashoka's missionaries took Buddhism to Ceylon, where the religion set down particularly deep roots.

Kushan India

Around 50 CE, the Kushans made northwestern India part of an empire stretching from the Ganges to the Aral Sea. They were a clan of the Yue Qi nomads who had overrun the Greek

ASHOKA

Born around 304 BCE and ruling from 268 to 233 BCE, Ashoka held sway over more of the Indian subcontinent than any ruler before him. After his death, it was not until the height of the Mughal Empire—almost 2,000 years later—that anyone controlled as much of India as he had. There is clear evidence of Ashoka's achievements as a ruler on the stone monuments inscribed with his sayings and orders. On one of these monuments is a sculpture of four outward facing lions, which has become the official symbol of modern India.

Ashoka was born into the Mauryan dynasty that ruled extensive areas in northern India. There are many legends about Ashoka's ancestry and childhood, and most of them are designed to emphasize his link to the Buddha. There are also many stories of Ashoka's youthful rivalry with his older brothers; according to one tale, he came to power by killing them all. Whether that is true or not, there is no doubt that, in the first eight years of his reign, Ashoka extend Mauryan power in a relentless series of campaigns across India, creating an empire that stretched from what is now Bangladesh in the east to what is now Iran in the west, and from the Himalayas in the north to include all but the southern tip of peninsular India. Ashoka's capital was Pataliputra, modern-day Patna in the state of Bihar.

Ashoka conquered the state of Kalinga on the east coast of India, probably around 261 BCE. The conquest was particularly bloody, and historians have estimated that 100,000 Kalingans were killed.

Apparently, the brutality of the conquest of Kalinga deeply affected Ashoka, and he adopted Buddhism as a response. One of his early wives, Devi, is said to have been a Buddhist who greatly influenced him.

There is no doubt that Ashoka tried to mold his empire into a coherent state with Buddhist principles at its core. He built numerous stupas (Buddhist shrines)—according to some sources, as many as 84,000 (traditionally, the number of ashes into which the body of the Buddha disintegrated). In line with Buddhist teachings, Ashoka forbade hunting except for food. He encouraged vegetarianism and herbal medicine and created a road system to facilitate pilgrimages to the most important Buddhist sites. He ended his policy of violent conquest, and Mauryan India enjoyed good relations with the Greek world. Ashoka also sent Buddhist missionaries out from India to all the surrounding states. Principles of tolerance for all religious groups were carved for all to see. That may have been common sense in a highly diverse empire, but it was unusual in the ancient world.

This Ashoka pillar at Sarnath, in the Indian state of Uttar Pradesh, was erected in the third century BCE.

This sandstone bust from the fourth century CE depicts an adherent of Jainism, the religion founded by Mahavira in the sixth century BCE.

CE, the united Kushan Empire was not restored.

The Kushan Empire was never highly centralized, and the king ruled through a host of dependent yaghbus (sub-kings). Kushan rulers used an eclectic range of titles, including maharaja (great king), rajatiraja (king of kings), the Greek title basileus (king), and kaisara (from the Latin *caesar*). They also instituted a cult of ruler worship and used the title devaputra (son of god). Kushan culture was equally eclectic, mixing Hellenistic, Indian, and central Asian styles. Kushan rulers were tolerant in matters of religion. Most of the early rulers were Buddhists, and the later ones were Hindus, but they all respected a wide range of Persian, Greek, and even Roman deities. The empire was always wealthy, prospering by its control of all the major trans-Asian overland trade routes. High-quality coinage was made by melting down gold Roman coins that flooded into the empire to pay for luxury goods such as Chinese silk.

The Kushans did not have a monopoly on east-west trade. By the first century CE, Mediterranean seafarers had discovered how to exploit the monsoon winds to sail across the Indian Ocean, bringing increased trade between the Roman Empire and southern India. The region's most valuable exports were spices, which the Romans paid for in gold. South Indian rulers did not issue their own coinage, and Roman coins circulated freely. The most powerful south Indian state in this period was Satavahanihara. However, the influx of wealth led to the formation of several small tribal kingdoms and cities in the region.

kingdom of Bactria around 135 BCE. The Kushan state was set up in Bactria around 25 CE by Kujula Kadphises, who invaded India and conquered Gandhara and the northern Sakas around 50 CE. Kujula's successor, Vima Kadphises (ruled c. 75–100 CE), conquered the Indus Valley and much of the Gangetic Plain. The empire reached its peak under Kanishka (ruled c. 100–130 CE), a devout Buddhist and a patron of the arts. Under Kanishka's successors, the Kushan Empire maintained its borders until the third century CE, when most of its western provinces were conquered by the Sassanian king Shapur I. Although the Kushans briefly regained their independence in the fourth century

See also:

The Buddha and Buddhism (volume 7, page 946) • Hinduism: The Religion of India (volume 7, page 932) • India in the Middle Ages (volume 7, page 960)

HINDUISM: THE RELIGION OF INDIA

TIME LINE

c. 2600 BCE

Earliest Indus Valley civilization develops.

c. 1500 BCE

Aryans enter India from central Asia; first Vedas composed.

c. 1200 BCE

Orally transmitted Vedas first written down.

c. 900 BCE

First Brahmanas composed as glosses to Vedas.

c. 800 BCE

Early Upanishads appended to Vedas.

c. 563 BCE

Birth of the Buddha.

c. 483 BCE

Death of the Buddha.

c. 200 BCE

Composition of Laws of Manu, early Hindu script.

c. 400 CE

Hinduism develops into approximately modern form.

The Aryans who migrated to India around 1500 BCE practiced forms of worship that were codified in the Vedas. Originally transmitted orally, the Vedas were written down around 1200 BCE. By the fifth century CE, they had inspired a new religion, Hinduism.

Hinduism developed over many centuries from the religion of the Aryan nomads who invaded and settled in the Indus River Valley in the northwestern Indian subcontinent around 1500 BCE. The faith of the Indo-European nomads is called Vedic religion, from the name of their holy books, the Vedas. Under a range of influences (including the rival faiths of Jainism and Buddhism) and a series of further invasions by European peoples between 200 BCE and 500 CE, Hinduism developed into approximately its modern form by around the fifth century CE.

Ancient Indians did not call their faith Hinduism—the word was not used until the 19th century CE, although it derives from the ancient Indo-European nomads' name for the Indus River. In ancient India, the faith was called Sanatana Dharma (Eternal Law), because it was said to have always existed. The Vedas, the scriptures of the Aryan nomads and their descendants, were classed not as *smriti* (recalled) but as *shruti* (heard); they were presented as the result of firsthand experience. Adherents believed that the faith had no founder because it had existed from the beginning of all things; it represented a statement of the natural law that governed material and spiritual reality and that applied—like the law of gravity—regardless of whether people were aware of it or paid respect to it.

Vedic religion

The warlike Aryans worshipped a range of nature deities and practiced a ritualized religion based on sacrifices performed by priests in sacred fire pits. The nomads' religion blended with that of the indigenous peoples of the region, descendants of the Indus Valley people, whose civilization had thrived from around 2600 to 2000 BCE and who, judging from the remains of cities at Mohenjo-Daro and Harappa (in modern Pakistan), worshipped the bull and a horned storm god believed to be a forerunner of Shiva, one of the principal deities of Hinduism.

The Vedic deities were primarily beneficent, and delivered prosperity to their worshippers. When natural disaster or other calamity struck, it was not through divine anger, as in the Judeo-Christian tradition, but through the actions of the gods' powerful enemies, the demons. The principal deities were male gods; goddesses were cast in supporting roles, reflecting the patriarchal organization of Aryan society.

The Mantrapureeswarar Temple at Kovilur, in Tamil Nadu, India, is dedicated to the Hindu god Shiva.

Seals such as this, found at Mohenjo-Daro and dating from no later than 2000 BCE, suggest that bulls were worshipped by the peoples of the Indus Valley civilization.

Many Vedic deities appear to have counterparts in the gods of other Indo-European religious cultures, notably the Zoroastrians in Persia and the ancient Greeks and Romans. Examples include the Aryan sky god Dyaus Pitar, who is directly comparable to the Roman Zeus Pater; Mitra, another sky god, known to the Persians as Mithra and, in the Roman Empire, the inspiration for a bull-slaying mystery cult; and the Vedic dawn goddess Usas, who is analogous to the Greek Eos. Varuna, the Vedic guardian of universal order, had counterparts in the Roman Uranus and the Zoroastrian Ahura Mazda.

Such apparent links between the religions of these different cultures have inspired speculation that they all had their origin in the religion practiced by the Indo-Europeans in their original homeland between the Black and Caspian seas before they embarked on the series of migrations to India, Iran, and Europe.

Order and sacrifice

According to the Aryans' Eternal Law, the universe was based on order (the Sanskrit word for which is *rita*) and creation began and life was sustained by sacrifice (*yajna*). Two creation myths alluded to in the hymns of the *Rig Veda* scripture state that the creator of the universe was a great being named Visva-karman (Maker of All), who brought all things into being by performing a ritual sacrifice. Visvakarman's sacrifice was celebrated and reenacted by priests when they gathered around the sacrificial flames in the fire pit and made offerings of grain, oil, and clarified butter.

THE VEDAS

The main sources of modern knowledge about the early development of Hinduism are the Aryan holy books known as the Vedas. The Vedas were probably transmitted orally for many years before they were first written in an archaic form of Sanskrit around 1200 BCE.

There are four Vedas: the *Rig Veda*, the *Yajur Veda*, the *Sama Veda*, and the *Atharva Veda*. The *Rig Veda* is principally a group of hymns; it contains the words of 1,028 religious songs in 10 books. The verses describe the delight of the Aryan nomads in the beautiful landscape of northwestern India and their apprehension of divine energy behind the different forms of nature. One hymn praises dawn and the Indus River: "We have crossed over to the other side of darkness. O, Dawn, you have prepared the way, you shine and smile … and

your lovely face has made us joyful….The Sun Goddess wakes the sleeping men to go forth. One goes to amuse himself; one goes to the assembly, deeply interested in the things he encounters. The Dawn has awakened all living beings…. Shimmering, sparkling, the Indus, the river richest in floods, brings its water to the surface like an untamed wild stallion."

The *Yajur Veda* is mainly a set of formulas to be chanted by priests while making sacrifices. Most of the *Sama Veda* is a collection of ritual chants used by *udgatri* (chanters). The *Atharva Veda* is a collection of magical incantations and spells. Of later origin than the other Vedas, the *Atharva Veda* was finally taken into the canon because it was used as a manual of ritual by brahmin priests.

Each of the Vedas is divided into four sections: the Samhitas, the Brahmanas, the Aranyakas, and the Upanishads. The Samhitas contain the poetic sections of each Veda and are used as hymns or mantras (sacred words). The Brahmanas are prose commentaries that explain liturgical details, particularly the origins and significance of sacrificial rituals. The Aranyakas and Upanishads investigate the nature and meaning of religious experience.

The Vedas were composed over many centuries. Although it is uncertain exactly when they were first written down, it is generally agreed that the oldest written parts of the Vedas, the hymns of the *Rig Veda*, date from between 1200 and 800 BCE. The Brahmanas and the earliest Aranyakas and Upanishads were written down between 800 and 500 BCE. The latest parts of the Veda are thought to have been written down between 500 and 200 BCE.

This illustration is taken from a manuscript of the Bhagavad Gita produced between the fifth and second centuries BCE.

Produced in India in the 18th century CE, this gouache illustration on paper depicts the Vedic god Varuna riding Makara, a crocodile-like sea monster.

from his feet, the sky from his head, the sun from his eyes, and the moon from his spirit. From Purusha's mouth came the thunder god, Indra, and the fire god, Agni; from his breath came the wind god, Vayu.

According to that story, all things were grounded in a single source—Purusha—and they all contained a part of Purusha within them. Central to religious life in the Vedic religion, and later in Hinduism, was the apprehension of the one in the many, of unity in multiplicity. Meditation (the focusing of attention while sitting quietly and the development of powerful inner concentration) was highly valued as a means of experiencing the divine unity that believers said had concealed itself within the multiplicity of the material world. In classical Hinduism, worshippers chose their family gods and goddesses from a wide variety of deities. They regarded the deities themselves as various personal aspects of the impersonal divine principle, *brahman*, which is found in all living beings.

Atman and brahman

Each of the four groups of ancient Indian scriptures—the *Rig Veda*, the *Yaju Veda*, the *Sama Veda*, and the *Atharva Veda* (see box, page 935)—contained a section of Upanishads (private lessons), which are thought to have been written in forest academies of spiritual living between around 800 and 200 BCE. The Upanishads (the name in Sanskrit means "sitting down near one's teacher") accompanied programs of spiritual learning at which young men trained through meditation and other disciplines under the guidance of their gurus (teachers).

The Upanishads recorded the results of an exploration of human modes of knowing. They taught that the deepest level of individual human consciousness, known as *atman* (self), was the same as

Another creation story in the *Rig Veda* cast the original man as Purusha, a vast being with 1,000 feet, 1,000 heads, and 1,000 eyes; the gods and wise men came forth from him and then pinned him down to be offered as a sacrifice. From clarified butter offered in the fire, the season of spring was created; from the burning of fuel, summer emerged, and the act of sacrifice created the fall. After the sacrifice, the gods and wise men made all the creatures of the earth from clarified butter, before the remainder of the universe was made from parts of Purusha—the earth

the universal divine consciousness, *brahman*; at the most profound level, every individual was united with God. *Atman* was *brahman*, and their identity could be experienced by any dedicated student who persevered in meditation.

Reincarnation and karma

Two other central notions in the developing faith of Hinduism were that every human action and even every thought had a consequence and that each individual soul survived physical death to be born again in a new body.

All people carried the results of past actions with them in the form of karma. The effects of a person's actions were played out both within one lifetime and across lifetimes. That explained birth inequalities in caste as well as varying physical and intellectual gifts. The theory of karma was effectively a translation of the physical law of cause and effect into the realm of religion and philosophy. It was neither a gloomy nor a passive concept. It offered hope and suggested that people could act in the present to shape the future. Those who changed their behavior could expect better circumstances in the future; if they changed the cause, they would bring about a change in the effect.

The goal for every individual was ultimately to achieve *moksha* (release)—freedom from the cycle of births and deaths. *Moksha* was achieved by a person's realization during his or her own current lifetime of the unity of the individual *atman* with the universal *brahman*. "Realizing" did not mean understanding the unity of *atman* and *brahman* intellectually, but experiencing and thereby "knowing" the unity. There were said to be three main paths to achieving *moksha*: through *bhakti*, devotion to a particular god; through *jnana-marga*, study and pursuit of knowledge; or through *karma-marga*, doing one's duty.

The development of ideas central to religious life in ancient India can be traced from the early hymns to the later parts of the Vedas, particularly the Upanishads. In the hymns of the *Rig Veda*, *brahman* meant "holy knowledge" or the hymns that encapsulated it. The earliest use of the term to refer to a universal divine consciousness occurs in the Brihadaranyaka, an early (possibly the

This likeness of Shiva in gouache on silk was produced in Nepal in the 18th century CE.

A sadhu (holy man) meditates outside a Hindu temple in Calcutta, India.

first) Upanishad from the ninth century BCE. There is no reference to reincarnation in the *Rig Veda* hymns; the concept is first introduced in the Brihadaranyaka and Chandogya Upanishads. Equally, in the Vedic period, animal sacrifice was common, and the notion of *ahimsa* (nonviolence) was not developed until the era of the early Upanishads.

The *trimurti*

The Hindu doctrine of *trimurti* taught that *brahman* took three principal divine forms, those of the gods Brahma, Vishnu, and Shiva. The idea of *trimurti* was developed early in the Common Era as a way of uniting the existing cults of those gods with the philosophical idea of *brahman*, the divine unity that had been expressed in the Upanishads.

Brahma, Vishnu, and Shiva were all originally Vedic gods. Brahma and Prajapati were hailed in the *Rig Veda* as creator gods, and in later Vedic tradition, they were combined into a single creative deity, Prajapati Brahma. Vishnu was a minor Vedic god, an ally of Indra, the thunder and war god. Shiva (Auspicious Lord) was the original name of Rudra (the Howler)—the Vedic god of cattle, healing, herbs, sacrifice, song, and storm—who was often also identified with Agni, the fire god.

Images of the *trimurti* generally depicted one god with three faces. The three gods were said to express distinct qualities of *brahman*: Brahma, the creator; Vishnu, the sustainer; and Shiva, the destroyer. Brahma was associated with earth (in which life generates), Vishnu with water (which sustains life), and Shiva with fire (the destroyer).

Brahma

Although there were thousands of temples dedicated to Shiva and Vishnu, there were very few devoted to Brahma. Brahma was said to be above popular worship, although a statue of him was sometimes included in temples to the other gods. Brahma was generally regarded as the creator god, a personification of the impersonal divinity, *brahman*. In some places, however, he was seen as the product of *brahman*'s interaction with a female divine energy, known as *maya* or *prakriti*. According to the Hindu scripture called the Laws of Manu (c. 200 BCE), when *brahman* was moved by a desire to create

This French engraving from the 18th century CE depicts the Hindu god Brahma.

the universe, it cast onto the primeval waters a seed that transformed naturally into a golden egg containing Brahma. When the egg split, Brahma used its two halves to make the earth and the sky, then created the other gods and all the animal and human inhabitants of the earth. In another account, told by the worshippers of Vishnu, at the dawn of time, Vishnu Padmanabha (Lotus Navel) slept on the primeval waters supported by Shesha, the thousand-headed serpent of eternity, and woke to find a red lotus plant emerging from his navel. The lotus supported Brahma, creator of the universe.

Brahma's creation was said to be cyclical. Each day in his life, or *kalpa*, was equivalent to 4,320 million years on earth. In the morning, Brahma created the universe; in the evening, he dissolved it into chaos once more, then slept before creating it again when he awoke. Each *kalpa* was divided into 1,000 ages known as *mahayugas*. That cycle was set within a larger one; 360 *kalpas* made a year in Brahma's life, and he himself was said to live for 100 years—the equivalent of 155,520 billion years on earth. At the end of that period, Brahma joined in the general dissolution, which was followed by 100 *kalpas* of chaos before the entire cycle began again with a new Brahma.

Artistic representations of Brahma showed him with yellow skin, riding a wild goose or seated on a lotus plant. His four heads and four arms stand for the four Vedas or holy books. In the *Mahabharata* and the *Ramayana* (epic poems), Brahma was cast as a grandfather, the chief of the gods, the most powerful of all sages, and the giver of boons or gifts. His consort was Sarasvati, the goddess of poetry and music, who was identified with Vac, the Vedic goddess of speech. Vac was said to have created Sanskrit, which was believed to be a sacred language, the closest humans could come to partaking in the divine music that took form in creation.

Vishnu

In the first centuries CE, Vishnu rose from obscurity among the Vedic gods to a position of prominence as a sustaining and benevolent deity. The stories of many minor gods and folkloric heroes were assimilated into his person. By sacred tradition, Vishnu was said to descend to earth when the universal law (*dharma*) was in danger of being swept away.

Vishnu had ten avatars (incarnations). His first avatar was as Matsya, half-man and half-fish, who saved Manu (a figure comparable to Noah in

This relief sculpture from the seventh century CE depicts the Hindu holy trinity of Brahma, Shiva, and Vishnu.

This wall painting of Vishnu is one of many images that adorn the lavishly decorated Sri Ranganathaswamy Temple in Srirangam, Tamil Nadu, India.

the Judeo-Christian tradition) from a great flood and destroyed a demon named Hayagriva (Horseneck), who had stolen the Vedas from Brahma. Matsya retrieved the Vedas and gave them back to Brahma. The second avatar was as Kurma, the turtle who supported the mountain with which the gods churned up the cosmic ocean and brought forth a number of sacred emanations, including the divine drink (*amrita*) and the goddess Lakshmi.

Vishnu's third avatar was as the bull Varaha, who killed a demon named Hiranyaksha (Eye of Gold), rescued the earth from the bed of the cosmic ocean, and again retrieved the holy Vedas. His fourth avatar was a lion, Narasimha, who

941

In this 19th-century-CE Indian album painting, the Hindu god Rama, on the back of the god Hanuman, shoots an arrow from a longbow in an effort to rescue his wife, Sita.

ASHRAMAS

The older Vedas identified three *ashramas* (goals of life) as follows: *artha* (wealth or material success), *kama* (sensual pleasure), and *dharma* (right social behavior). The Vedas also described the obligations that a person was expected to meet in three stages of life: first, as a *brahmachari* (student); second, as a *grihastha* (householder), when he fulfilled duties to spouse, family, and local community; and third, as *vanaprastha*, a hermit or denizen of the forest who withdrew from material concerns to concentrate on religious matters. The Upanishads described a fourth stage, that of the *sannyasin* (renouncer), who foreswore all obligations and focused on achieving *moksha* (release from the cycle of birth and death).

killed another wicked demon, Hiranya-kashipu. In his fifth avatar, Vishnu took the form of a dwarf named Vamana; he came into being to thwart the wicked plotting of an earthly king named Bali. Bali had taken possession of the universe, including the abode of the gods, but Vamana tricked him into giving them back. He persuaded Bali to agree to give him as much land as he could encompass in three strides. Vamana then abandoned the body of the dwarf and grew enormously so that his three steps measured out the entire universe, including the home of the gods. Bali gave the lands back and was made the god of the underworld.

In his sixth avatar—as a priest named Parashurama—Vishnu defeated a 100-armed warrior who was undermining *dharma* by threatening the brahmins (priests). In his seventh avatar, Vishnu was

the god Rama, as described in the *Ramayana*. In his eighth avatar, Vishnu became the god Krishna, as detailed in the *Mahabharata*. Vishnu's ninth avatar was as the historical Buddha, Prince Gautama, the founder of Buddhism. Vishnu's tenth and final avatar lay in the future, as Kalki, who would arrive to end creation either as a warrior on a white horse or as the horse itself.

Vishnu was usually represented with dark-blue skin, riding the golden-bodied man-bird Garuda, who, in the Vedas, brought nectar from heaven to earth. Vishnu had one empty hand (as a giver of gifts), one hand holding a discus (symbolizing the sun) or a wheel (the cycle of births and deaths), another hand holding a conch shell (from which the elements were created), and the fourth hand holding a lotus (symbolizing his creativity).

Rama and Krishna

The exploits of Vishnu's seventh avatar, Rama, were probably based on those of a historical prince from around 1000 to 700 BCE. The story of how Rama rescued his wife, Sita, after she was kidnapped by the demon king of Sri Lanka was told first in the *Mahabharata* before being developed in the later *Ramayana*. By the start of the Common Era, the figure of Rama had been incorporated into the religious tradition of the god Vishnu and established as one of his avatars. Rama became a very popular god in his own right, revered as an exemplar of loyalty and bravery. He was usually depicted with blue skin and wearing a tall cap.

Likewise, the story of Krishna, which told how the god defeated Kamsa, the evil ruler of a northern Indian people named the Yadavas, was a blend of historical fact and religious tradition. The factual elements were derived from the life of a historical hero of the Yadavas and combined with tales of a flute-playing forest god of southern India. Seen as an avatar of Vishnu, Krishna was also a very popular god in his own right. As an infant, Krishna was sent away from the court to be raised in the safety of a forest village. There, he dallied with the *gopis*, the wives of the local cowherd, and in particular with his favorite, Radha. Krishna was often depicted with blue-black skin, wearing a headdress of peacock

This statuette depicts Shiva dancing.

feathers and playing his flute. During his forest childhood, Krishna killed a five-headed snake demon named Kaliya.

Shiva

Shiva united many contradictory qualities in a single person. He was creator as well as destroyer, both benign and malevolent. He gave expression to the anger of the avenger as well as to the benevolence of the restorer. He was celebrated both as an ascetic mystic and as a great lover.

Shiva had five main aspects. The first was as a holy man, seated on Mount Kailasa in the Himalayas, who, by the power of his meditation, generated the *tapas* (energy that sustained the universe). The second aspect was as the four-armed god Nataraja, who danced on top of the dwarf of ignorance while holding the fire of destruction and new life and playing the drum of time and creation. Shiva-Nataraja is often depicted with one right hand raised to indicate "Have no fear" and one left hand pointed at the foot he has lifted out of the circle of fire that surrounds him, which offers his devotees escape from the cycle of birth and death. Shiva's third aspect was as a fertility god in the form of the *lingam*, a stone pillar representing the penis and the creative potentiality of life. The fourth aspect was as Bhairava (defeater of

943

EPICS OF HINDU LITERATURE

The two great epic poems of India, the *Mahabharata* and the *Ramayana*, are revered by Hindus as the most sacred scriptures. With 200,000 lines, the *Mahabharata* is the world's longest poem, some seven times longer than the two great epics of ancient Greece, the *Iliad* and the *Odyssey*, combined.

According to legend, the *Mahabharata* was first transcribed by a priest named Vsaya, following the dictation of the elephant god, Ganesh. In truth, it is a virtual encyclopedia of folklore, astronomy, law, geography, theories of government, mathematics, and philosophy assembled by priests and poets between 300 BCE and 400 CE. Its main narrative concerns the war between two sets of cousins, the Pandavas and the Kauravas. It contains the Bhagavad Gita (c. 200 BCE), a 700-verse poem that recounts the conversation between the Pandava warrior Arjuna and his charioteer, who reveals himself to be the god Krishna (an incarnation of Vishnu). Krishna instructs Arjuna in the nature of ultimate reality and in how to gain release from *samsara* (the cycle of birth and death) by acting without self-interest in accordance with one's duty (*dharma*), by pursuing knowledge, and by demonstrating *bhakti* (devotion) to a personal god.

The *Ramayana,* a 48,000-line poem probably compiled between 200 BCE and 200 CE, tells the story of a prince named Rama who set out to rescue his wife, Sita, after she had been kidnapped from Sri Lanka by a demon king named Ravana. Rama succeeded in his mission with the assistance of the monkey god, Hanuman.

*This illustration from a 16th-century-CE edition of the **Mahabharata** shows a battle between the **Pandavas and the Kauravas.***

demons) or Buteshvara (god of ghosts). Shiva's fifth aspect was as a medicine god, a holy shepherd of the souls of men and a gatherer of healing herbs. Depicted with a third eye, he saved his devotees from destruction by using his hair to break the fall of the sacred Ganges River when it was released from heaven.

The goddesses

The worship of a mother goddess had ancient origins in India, dating from at least the third millennium BCE, when people of the Indus Valley civilization made statuettes of wide-hipped women that are thought to have been used in fertility rites. Vedic religion, however, was dominated by gods. Goddesses generally had subordinate roles, although several of them were celebrated in Vedic hymns. Among the most prominent were Sarasvati, Ganges, and Yamuna (three river goddesses), Usha (the dawn goddess), Vac (the goddess of speech and poetry), and Aditi (upholder of the sky and sustainer of existence). In the early centuries of the Common Era, however, goddesses achieved independent prominence as objects of worship.

The principal goddess—known either as Shakti (from the Sanskrit for "energy") or as Devi (from the Sanskrit *div*, meaning "to shine")—took many forms. All the principal gods were worshipped alongside their goddess consorts: Vishnu was accompanied by Lakshmi; Brahma had Sarasvati; Krishna had Radha; Rama had Sita. All these goddesses were seen as aspects of the one great goddess. Mythologically, the supreme female deity was conceived primarily as Parvati, the daughter of the mountain Himalaya, who carried the creative power of womankind. Parvati became the consort of Shiva, in which role she appeared as a woman of incomparable beauty. However, she had two other manifestations: the terrifying forms of

Durga and Kali. Durga was Shiva's spouse when he appeared as Bhairava (defeater of demons), and she was created by the gods to kill the buffalo demon, Mahishasura. When Parvati took the form of Kali, she appeared as a black-skinned goddess with a necklace of skulls. Kali was a bloodthirsty deity who delighted in receiving animal sacrifices.

This sculpture on the exterior of a Hindu temple at Madurai, India, depicts the god Ganesh.

See also:

India in the Middle Ages (volume 7, page 960) • India's First Civilizations (volume 7, page 918)

THE BUDDHA AND BUDDHISM

Derived in part from the Indian holy books, the four Vedas, Buddhism became established in the fifth century BCE during the lifetime of its founder, Siddharta Gautama. It then spread throughout India, China, Thailand, and many other parts of Asia.

Buddhism is often said to be a way of life rather than a conventional religion. It has had a profound effect on the history of Asia, partly because the beliefs of Buddhists are very influential but also because Buddhist monks and nuns, organized in monasteries, played an important role in many societies during the ancient and medieval periods.

Siddharta Gautama, known as the Buddha (Enlightened One) and founder of the philosophical-religious system of Buddhism, was born around 563 BCE in northern India. His father was chief of the Sakya clan, which led to the Buddha being called Sakyamuni (Sage of the Sakyas). Siddharta and his fellow Sakyas were members of the kshatriya, an Indian caste established by Aryan (Indo-European) invaders in the second millennium BCE. The kshatriyas were warrior aristocrats and rulers; above them in the hierarchy were the brahmins (priests), while below them were the vaishyas (farmers and traders, which made up most of the general population) and the shudras (laborers, craftsmen, and servants).

By the time of Siddharta's birth, most of the Vedas—the holy books of the Aryan peoples—had already been composed. The works included the Upanishads, which proposed that the individual soul was eternally connected to a universal divinity residing at the core of all living beings. A key part of the Aryans' Vedic religion was belief in the centrality of ritual sacrifices performed by brahmin priests. Another important element of the religion as it had developed by the sixth century BCE was the belief in reincarnation, the idea that human souls entered a new body after death and lived life again. Individuals were said to go through a cycle of many births and deaths. According to legend, the Buddha himself declared shortly after his birth: "This is my final existence."

The sixth century BCE was a time of socioeconomic and cultural transition in northern India. The use of iron was increasing, trading cities were being established along the Ganges River, and commerce was being transformed as merchants adopted silver and copper coinage on the Persian model. A religious upheaval was approaching too. New spiritual teachers and movements emerged to compete with the religion of the brahmin priests, challenging the authority of the Vedas and objecting to the Vedic religion's ritualistic nature, its sacrifices, and its elitism. On the crest of the radical new wave were Siddharta

This golden statue is one of many effigies of the Buddha in Thailand, where Buddhism is the majority religion.

JAINISM

In the sixth century BCE, around the same time as the Buddha was teaching the way to enlightenment, another major religious teacher was also at work in northern India. Born into the kshatriya caste, Vardhamana chose a path of extreme asceticism, living without possessions (even clothes) as a wandering holy man for 12 years until he achieved a state of pure and perfect perception called *kevala jnana*. Vardhamana—also known as Mahavira (Sanskrit meaning "Great Hero")—taught that people should seek *ahimsa* (nonviolence) in all things. He argued that to live a pure and clean life, people should make five vows of renunciation: not to kill, not to lie, not to be greedy, not to take sexual pleasure, and not to be attached. Vardhamana is widely regarded as the founder of the religion of Jainism, although according to Jain tradition, he was merely the last of 24 teachers who established the faith. Today, there are 4.2 million Jains, and most of them live in India.

Although Jainism developed out of the same religious ferment and rejection of Vedic practice as Buddhism, it adopted many aspects of what later became Hinduism. What it always maintained was its intense respect for all forms of life and its refusal to kill any living beings.

Gautama and Vardhamana—also known as Mahavira (Great Hero; c. 599–527 BCE)—the founder of Jainism.

Siddharta Gautama

Siddharta Gautama was married at age 16 to a cousin from a neighboring country. The wedding was arranged to promote a political alliance. Siddharta's wife gave birth to a son, assuring the continuation of the dynasty. Siddharta himself led a very sheltered life within his elite social circle. According to Buddhist tradition, it was not until he was 29 years of age that he first witnessed human suffering. The sight appalled him and inspired him to abandon his privileged life and embark on a search for enlightenment (the realization of eternal truth).

Siddharta studied with two yoga masters and devoted himself to meditation. He tried extreme sensory self-denial, but after six years, he rejected asceticism on the grounds that it had not led to his enlightenment. By that stage, he had already gathered five disciples, but they abandoned him when he gave up asceticism. He now chose a middle path, one of moderation, following a lifestyle that was neither ascetic nor self-indulgent.

Around 528 BCE, while sitting in meditation beneath a tree in the forest of Bodh Gaya (in the modern Indian state of Bihar), Siddharta reached the goal he sought. According to tradition, he meditated all night, ridding himself of his "outflows" (ignorance and desire) and moving through rising levels of consciousness until he understood the Four Noble Truths and attained the Great Enlightenment. He then announced that he was the Buddha.

According to Buddhist tradition, Siddharta met the god Brahma (a creator in the pantheon of the Vedic religion and later a major Hindu deity, often seen as grandfather of the gods and the source of ultimate wisdom). Brahma is said to have convinced the Buddha to make his teachings known out of compassion for humankind. The Buddha traveled to Benares (modern Varanasi), a city on the banks of the Ganges River in northeastern India. At nearby Sarnath, he gave his first sermon. His audience was the group of five disciples who had abandoned him when he gave up the ascetic path. He taught the Four Noble Truths about the human condition and outlined the Eightfold Path as a means of escaping human suffering.

The Buddha spent the next 45 years as an itinerant teacher, gathering followers and establishing sanghas (monasteries). His first disciples were the five ascetics who had previously abandoned him but rejoined him at Sarnath. Their ranks

THE BUDDHA'S GREAT RENUNCIATION

According to Buddhist tradition, one day, Siddharta was riding out with his shield-bearer, Chanda, when he was struck by the strange appearance of one particular passerby. "Who is that fellow with white hair, dull eyes, and trembling hands?" he asked.

"Why, it is an old man," Chanda replied. "He was once a child who lay at his mother's breast and later a young man full of life. But now his bloom has faded, and he has lost his strength."

"How can a person be happy when he knows that he will soon be old and useless?" Siddharta wondered aloud.

Shortly afterward, Siddharta saw another man sitting beside the road, as if washed up by the river of life. "What is wrong with him?" he asked Chanda.

"He is ill," Chanda explained. "The organs of his body have failed. We are all subject to physical malfunctions."

After the second encounter, Chanda used his whip to hurry the horses along in an attempt to spare his master from being forced to witness any more unpleasant

sights. However, they had not gone much farther when they encountered a funeral procession.

Siddharta had never seen such a thing before. "What are those people carrying among the flowers?" he asked Chanda.

The shield-bearer gently replied: "They are accompanying a corpse. That man's limbs are stiff and his thoughts have left him; he no longer lives. His joys and his sorrow are over. Everything must die; it is not possible to escape death."

Those encounters with old age, illness, and death helped form Siddharta's view that suffering was the inescapable experience of humankind. When he subsequently met an itinerant ascetic holy man, who showed himself to be serene in his rejection of earthly attachments, Siddharta decided to try that way of life himself. He left his wife, his son, and his comfortable life in the palace in order to seek the truth as a mendicant. His decision is celebrated by Buddhists as the Great Renunciation.

This ninth-century-CE Chinese painting shows Siddharta's four encounters on the road to his Great Renunciation.

This temple at Sarnath in Uttar Pradesh, India, is built on the site of the deer park where, according to tradition, the Buddha preached his first sermon.

were swelled by converts from the Buddha's own family: his father, his wife, and other relatives. Following the death of his father, the Buddha's stepmother also became a disciple. When their number reached 60, the Buddha sent his disciples out to spread his teaching along the Ganges Valley, between the cities of Allahabad and Patna in northeastern India.

When he was around 80 years old, the Buddha traveled to Kushinagara in Nepal. There, around 483 BCE, after a brief illness said to have been caused by eating tainted pork, he came to the end of his bodily life. Amid extensive ceremonies, his body was cremated by a local prince. According to Buddhist tradition, the founder's ashes were divided into 84,000 units and distributed among the main followers, who installed them in stupas (relic shrines). The Buddha had become the Tathagata (he who has reached the state of perfection).

The teachings of the Buddha

The Buddha's teachings are collectively known as the dharma, or the way to enlightenment. Basic to the dharma are the Four Noble Truths and the steps of the Eightfold Path.

The first noble truth was that all life was *dukkha* (suffering). The Buddha said that birth was suffering, aging was suffering, illness was suffering, death was suffering; being separated from what was pleasing was suffering, as was having what was displeasing or not having what one wanted. His point was not that suffering was a part of life; it was that suffering *was* life; the whole of existence was suffering, and the suffering was unrelieved even by death, because death was followed by rebirth.

The second noble truth was that all suffering came from ignorance. Desire, or the craving for and attachment to the pleasures of life, was caused by that ignorance. The third noble truth was that suffering could be ended by eliminating ignorance and desire. The fourth noble truth outlined the way to end suffering by following the Eightfold Path, which comprised right views, right resolve, right speech, right action, right livelihood, right effort, right mindfulness, and right concentration. Making the right choices on the path would lead a seeker toward morality, wisdom, and mindful concentration. The last named, also known as *samadhi*, could be achieved through meditation.

The Buddha also taught that aspirants to enlightenment should follow the Middle Way, avoiding the two extremes of indulgence in sensual pleasure and self-castigation through painful habits. The Middle Way opened the aspirant's eyes to understanding and brought peace, because it was able to deliver wisdom and truth.

The Buddha made no claim to divinity. He taught that any human who followed his teachings could achieve enlightened, as he had. Enlightenment was a matter of individual human effort and could be reached by following the Eightfold Path and by practicing meditation. According to tradition, the Buddha said: "Seek in the impersonal for the eternal man and having sought him out look inward—you are Buddha." He explained that he had simply found the path and was now showing it to others;

Built between the first century BCE and the first century CE, the great stupa at Sanchi is one of many such structures erected in India to mark the holy sites of Buddhism.

This Tibetan scroll painting from the 18th century CE depicts the Buddha cutting his hair.

he was like a physician who saw the causes and treatment of a disease—the disease of suffering in existence. The physician made recommendations, but the healing of the patient depended on his or her own efforts.

The Buddha rejected the many gods of Vedic religion, although he did not specifically deny their existence. He taught that rather than being exalted beings in control of human fate, they were bound, like humans, in the cycle of births and deaths called *samsara* and were liable to be reborn as lower creatures. He

did not believe that there was any value in offering prayers or making sacrifices to those deities.

Impermanence and karma

The Buddha denied the existence of an enduring individual self or soul such as that called *atman* in the Upanishads and in Hinduism. He taught the doctrine of *anatman* (no soul), according to which people were made up of impermanent combinations of elements or bundles, known as *skandhas*. The *skandhas* includ-ed the body, the emotions, perception, volition, and consciousness. The idea of an immortal individual personality was seen as a damaging illusion that led to self-centeredness, craving, and suffering. *Abutya* (impermanence) was, the Buddha taught, just as fundamental to human existence as *dukkha* (suffering).

According to the doctrine of *pratitya-samutpada* (dependent origin), the make-up of an individual was determined by a chain of causation, each link in the chain arising from the previous one and giving rise to the next one. The first link was ignorance, the cause of human suffering. Ignorance led to the will to live, a prerequisite for the consciousness of the mind and the senses. The mind determined the "name and form," the visible and invisible qualities of the human being. The senses permitted contact with the outside world, and such contact led to perception, then to desire, and then to attachment to existence. From existence came birth, old age, death, and rebirth. In Buddhist teaching, there was a connection between life and life, but not in the Hindu sense of the transmigration of an individual *atman*, because, according to the Buddha, the individual soul was only a transitory aggregate of *skandhas*.

Pratityasamutpada is related to the Buddha's concept of karma (act or deed), because it acted between one bodily

This marble tablet, inscribed with the Tripitaka (the oldest Buddhist canon), was carved in the 19th century CE and is housed in a Buddhist pagoda in Mandalay, Myanmar.

existence and another. A person's karma would determine his or her personal attributes, appearance, intelligence, caste, and even species in rebirth. The Buddha said that there were five destinations: (1) rebirth in hell, (2) coming into existence as a starving spirit, (3) being born as an animal, (4) coming back again as a human, and (5) taking form as a god. Karma was unavoidable, not a matter of divine judgment but the effect of a cause.

The initial conditions of present life were determined by a person's past actions, but his or her actions in the present were not fated or predetermined. He or she could choose freely, modifying behavior and changing karma. It was essential to adopt the four right attitudes: compassion, kindness, sympathetic joy, and equanimity. The Buddha also offered five moral precepts: people should not kill, steal, use hurtful language, indulge in sexual misconduct, or use intoxicants.

Nirvana

The Buddha taught that the goal in life was to achieve release from karma and liberation from *samsara* by reaching nirvana (literally, "to blow out"). To the Buddha, nirvana meant a condition in which the fires of desire, hatred, and ignorance had been extinguished and the individual had achieved complete detachment. Nirvana was not annihilation but the attainment of the highest form of consciousness.

The Buddha reputedly refused to answer questions about the nature of the universe or about nirvana, considering it pointless to think about those things. He spoke instead about how nirvana could be reached. He considered it a waste of time to seek the beginning and end of things, explaining: "A religious life does not depend on the question of whether the world is infinite or finite, nor whether or not we exist after death.... When the fire goes out, do you ask yourself if it has gone to the north or to the south, to the east or to the west?"

A Buddhist monk rests outside the royal palace in Bangkok, Thailand. More than 90 percent of modern Thailand's population of 65 million people are Buddhists.

Buddhist monasteries

By the fifth century BCE, there was a well-established tradition in India of holy men who traveled the country in good weather and took refuge in forest clearings during the annual monsoon. The Buddha himself is said to have gone on a forest retreat in a secluded spot near Benares (modern Varanasi). In time, the various centers originally built as refuges from the rain became *viharas* (permanent Buddhist monasteries).

The Buddha taught that, although anyone could attain nirvana by following the Eightfold Path, people freed of worldly cares had a better chance of succeeding. He did not suggest that a monk or a nun was better equipped than a lay person to reach that goal, but he did point out that life in a sangha (monastic order) provided a way to achieve it. Monasteries were open to men and women alike, from any walk of life and from any caste, although escaped slaves, debtors, soldiers, and people in the service of a sovereign were excluded.

Buddhist monks and nuns were subjected to strict discipline, which varied considerably from one tradition to another. No monk or nun was permitted to have sexual relations, steal, kill or pretend to have supernatural power. Offenses were punishable by expulsion from the order. Joining an order was easy; novitiates shaved their head, put on a habit, and made a declaration in the presence of an older monk or nun. The ordination was a ceremonial occasion that involved extensive questioning and culminated in the assumption of a new name to symbolize a break with the person's old life.

Sanghas depended on the laity, because the monks and nuns were unproductive. That tradition had many practical repercussions. Because the greatest benefactor of sanghas was often the sovereign, Buddhism became a part of the political world. Although monks and nuns were allowed to own virtually nothing, the monastic community as a collective could accept generous donations, particularly of land. A sangha could own land worked by lay farmers who gave part of the harvest to the monks. At certain times, monks also engaged in commercial activity. Sanghas were often situated around relic shrines and became pilgrimage centers. Some sanghas aggressively demanded donations and became a burden on the districts in which they were located.

Splits among Buddhists

In the centuries following the Buddha's death around 483 BCE, the community of his followers split into a number of sects. Ancient Buddhist texts refer to 18 schools, but in chronicles, there are references to no fewer than 30 different groups. The Buddhists were still united when they met in a first council of followers at Rajagriha (modern Rajgir) in northeastern India, seeking to agree on what the Buddha had said and to record his words. However, a split occurred at a second council in Vaishali (in the modern

This stupa at Benares (modern Varanasi), India, was built around 500 CE.

state of Bihar) around 383 BCE. A group of monks in the Vajjian Confederacy had strayed from accepted practice by using money and drinking wine, and although the council censured their activities, the condemnation was not unanimous. The liberal Mahasanghikas (Great Assembly) split from the more traditional Sthaviras (Elders).

The Mahasanghikas had come to an understanding of the nature of the Buddha that was different from that of their fellow Buddhists. Rather than regarding the Buddha as a human who had found enlightenment, they argued that he was an eternal being and that Siddharta Gautama had been created as an apparition of the transcendent Buddha to help people understand him. That concept was important in the later Mahayana form of Buddhism.

The Sthaviras later became known as Theravadins. From their original base in southern India, they spread to Ceylon (Sri Lanka) in the third century BCE. Their form of Buddhism was known as Theravada (Way of the Elders) or Shravakayana (Vehicle of the Disciples) by those who followed or revered it, and

as Hinayana (Lesser Vehicle) by those who did not.

To followers of Theravada, it was essential to enter a monastic order to follow the Eightfold Path properly; lay people were unlikely to attain enlightenment and achieve nirvana but could nevertheless gain merit by supporting the monks financially. Monks who attained enlightenment were called *arhats* (saints). Theravadans worshipped the Buddha through the cult of stupas, dome-shaped stone shrines built to house Buddhist relics.

Around the first century CE, another major school of Buddhism developed. Known as the Mahayana (Greater Vehicle), its followers accepted the claim of the Mahasanghikas that the human Buddha was an earthly manifestation of a transcendent heavenly Buddha. The Mahayana Buddhists proposed that the Buddha had a three-bodied aspect. The first body (the body of essence) was formless, unchanging and absolute, the ultimate consciousness, the essential Buddha. The second body (the body of communal bliss) took a godlike form in the heavens. The third body (the body of transformation) was a human form taken

This statue of the Buddha is located at Borobudur on the island of Java.

A worshipper burns incense and prays at a Buddhist temple in Bangkok, Thailand.

to show humans the truth. Siddharta Gautama was only one of countless three-bodied Buddhas.

Unlike the Theravada Buddhists, the followers of Mahayana believed that a lay person had as much chance as a monk of achieving enlightenment. Mahayana Buddhists also disagreed with Thera-vadans over the ultimate goal of the Buddhist, suggesting that it should not be to become an *arhat* (saint) but to become a *bodhisattva*, an individual who attained enlightenment but then chose not to enter nirvana, in order to work for the enlightenment of others on earth.

Ritual and prayer, often chanted, were important in Mahayana Buddhist worship. Statues and portraits of the Buddha and of *bodhisattvas* were objects of devotion in temples and private homes. Theravada Buddhists viewed the Tripitaka (Three Baskets) as the words of

the Buddha himself and revered it as an absolute authority, but the Mahayanists considered the Three Baskets to be temporary teachings, not invalid but not final either. They accepted other *sutras* (scriptures), including the Prajnaparamita (Perfection of Wisdom; 100 BCE–150 CE), the Avatamsaka (Garland; known from Chinese translations in the second century CE), and the Lankavatara (Appearance of the Teaching in Lanka; from the fourth century CE onward). This last one is said to be the record of a sermon preached by the Buddha in the mythical city of Lanka.

A Buddhist empire

A strong missionary drive was always part of the Buddhist tradition. The Buddha told his followers to "go forth ... for the help of the many, for the well-being of the many, out of compassion for the

957

This statuette, carved in Burma (modern Myanmar) in the 12th or 13th century CE, depicts the Buddha seated on a lotus throne beneath a tree. Around him are scenes from his life.

gion, converting to Buddhism around 260 BCE. He initiated social reforms, ordering the construction of medical centers, the digging of wells, and the planting of banyan trees to provide shade for travelers. He also set up veterinary centers, forbade the cruel treatment of animals, and regulated their slaughter. Ashoka spread Buddhism with all the zeal of a new convert; he built monasteries and shrines and had the sayings of the Buddha engraved on rocks and monuments. He sent officials throughout his lands to monitor the application of a code of conduct based on *ahimsa* (nonviolence) and mutual respect. The reign of Ashoka marked the beginning of the spread of Buddhism to other Asian countries beyond India.

Spreading the word

Ashoka's son, Mahendra, became a monk and, around 250 BCE, took Theravada Buddhism to Ceylon (Sri Lanka), where it has remained the dominant religion into the modern era. According to tradition, it was carried from Ceylon to Burma (Myanmar) around the same time, but the first evidence of it there appeared in the fifth century CE. By the sixth century CE, Buddhism had spread to Thailand, where it became the national religion.

In the sixth century CE, a form of Mahayana Buddhism was introduced into China as Ch'an Buddhism (from *dhyana*, the Sanskrit word for the enlightenment achieved through meditation). Ch'an Buddhism thrived in Japan, where it was known as Zen Buddhism, from around the 12th century CE. Zen Buddhism proposed that enlightenment was achievable by anyone and that the best way to reach it was by suddenly

world." Nevertheless, the influence of the new philosophy did not extend far beyond northeastern India until the third century BCE, when Ashoka, king of the Mauryan dynasty, became a convert and spread its teachings throughout his lands.

In 261 BCE, Ashoka seized lands in the state of Kalinga on the east coast of India. It was a brutal conquest, and Ashoka was later overcome by remorse for the suffering he had caused. He renounced warfare and the Vedic reli-

bursting through patterns of habitual thought. Zen had a great influence on the culture of Japan.

In the seventh century CE, another school of Buddhism developed in northern India from a blend of the Mahayana tradition and folkloric beliefs. Known as the Vajrayana (Diamond Vehicle) or Tantric Buddhism, it taught the use in religious life of esoteric mystical-magical texts called *tantras* and secret rituals called *mudras*. Vajrayana arose around the same time as a similar tantric movement in Hinduism. Vajrayana is characterized by the use of mandalas (maps that symbolize spiritual reality) and the mantra (a sacred syllable chanted as a focus for meditation). Vajrayana was introduced in Tibet in 747 CE by the Indian monk Padmasambhava, and it became the predominant religion in that country. Around the 15th century CE, Tibetan monks began to regard the lamas (abbots) of their monasteries as reincarnations of *bodhisattvas* and the principal one, the Dalai Lama, as the ruler of the country. The theocracy was ended when China seized Tibet in 1951 CE.

Amidism (Pure Land Doctrine) was another school of Mahayana Buddhism to emerge. It began in India but first came to prominence in China around the fourth century CE and was carried to Japan around the ninth century CE. It emphasized belief in a transcendent, compassionate Buddha known in Japanese as Amida. Followers were taught that merely by believing in Amida, by hearing or repeating his name, they could be reborn in his western paradise, the Pure Land.

While Buddhism prospered in various forms outside of India, it declined in the land of its origin. Beginning in the fourth century CE, Buddhism came under pressure from a revival of interest in the religion of the brahmins, which was developing into classical Hinduism. The most

powerful blow to Buddhism in India, however, came from Islam. Islamic Turks conquered northern India in the 12th century CE, pushing Buddhism into peripheral areas. However, in the 20th century CE, Buddhism enjoyed a significant revival as the Indian scholar and political leader Bhimrao Ramji Ambedkar (1891–1956 CE), who was born into the lowest stratum of the Indian caste system, converted around 3.5 million of his fellow untouchables to the teachings of Buddha.

With China occupying Tibet, the Dalai Lama, Tenzin Gyatso, was forced into exile in 1959 CE.

See also:

Hinduism: The Religion of India (volume 7, page 932) • India's First Civilizations (volume 7, page 918)

INDIA IN THE MIDDLE AGES

I ndia underwent momentous political changes as struggles for territory saw the rise and fall of numerous dynasties throughout the subcontinent. The period was also marked by the further spread of three religions: Buddhism, Hinduism, and Islam.

In the fourth century CE, the Gupta dynasty built an empire in northern, central, and western India. The earlier Mauryan dynasty, which was at its height under the Buddhist ruler Ashoka (c. 268–233 BCE), collapsed in the second century BCE, and 500 years of political instability had followed. The Guptas came to power at a time when the Kushan dynasty, which was of central Asian origin, was losing power in the north and northwest of India.

The Gupta dynasty was Indian in origin and probably came from Bengal. It rose to power in the fourth century CE under Chandragupta I, a chieftain from Magadha (part of modern Bihar), who gained control of lands farther north by marriage. He subsequently extended his territory west as far as Kausambi (modern Allahabad). Chandragupta I took the title maharajadhiraja (king of kings) around 320 CE. His son, Samudra Gupta, was a great conqueror who, between 335 and 375 CE, built on his father's solid foundations. The Guptas won control of the major portion of northern India, while Assam, Nepal, Punjab, and enormous parts of the south paid tribute to them. Samudra Gupta's achievements were recorded in an inscription on one of the pillars originally raised by Ashoka at Kausambi. Samudra Gupta called himself chakra-vartin (king of the world). After defeating 9 kings in northern India and 12 kings in southern India, he performed a prestigious *ashwamedha yajna* (horse sacrifice) to celebrate his success.

The Gupta Empire reached its peak under Samudra Gupta's son, Chandragupta II (ruled 375–414 CE). At the height of its power, the empire extended from the northern border of modern Pakistan to the mouth of the Narmada River and from the mouth of the Indus River to the mouth of the Ganges River. The capital was Pataliputra (modern Patna). Chandragupta II called himself vikramaditya (sun of valor).

The golden age of the Guptas

The period of Gupta rule, which lasted until the sixth century CE, was a golden age in northern India. The arts and architecture flourished, and the religion derived from the Vedas and the ritual sacrifices of the brahmins began to develop into classical Hinduism. Under the Guptas, who particularly revered the sustaining god Vishnu and called themselves paramabhagavata (the principal worshippers of Vishnu), the first great stone temples were erected in northern India. Also around this time, the mother goddess became a popular object of worship, notably in the form of Durga, her incarnation as a consort of Shiva.

Among other developments under the Guptas, the traditional Hindu practice of performing acts of worship in front of an image of a chosen god or goddess became established, while temple design began to take new forms that remained fashionable for centuries. The classic temple structure of the period was a great tower (representing the home of the gods in Mount Meru) set in a courtyard with a central shrine that housed the image of the deity. Within the temples, artists painted splendid murals, and sculptors carved great sculptures. Most of the 28 rock-cut cave monuments at Ajanta in the state of Maharashtra were made during the Gupta era.

The Guptas oversaw a great flowering of literature in Sanskrit. The leading author of the age was the poet Kalidasa (see box, page 963). Building on the foundations laid by the sages of ancient India, scientists made many great breakthroughs in mathematics and astronomy.

This wall painting from the Ajanta caves depicts the Mahakapi Jataka (or Great Monkey King), a figure from Buddhist mythology. The painting dates to either the fifth or sixth century CE.

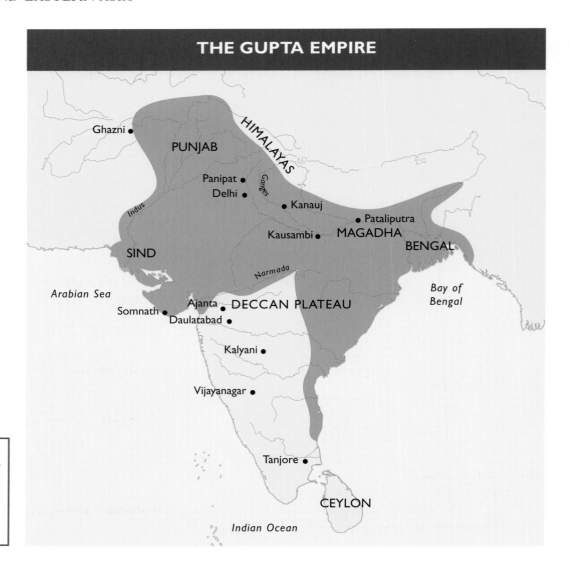

THE GUPTA EMPIRE

KEY

Extent of the
Gupta Empire
by 410 CE

The most famous scientist of the period, Aryabhata (c. 476–550 CE), developed the use of algebra and made significant advances in trigonometry (the study of triangles). He also calculated the length of the solar year, with extraordinary accuracy, to 365.3586 days and determined that the earth was not stationary but spinning on its axis.

The fall of the Guptas

In the second half of the fifth century CE, hordes of warlike central Asian nomads began incursions into India from the northwest, just as the Aryans had done more than 1,000 years previously. Little is known of the new invaders, who were called the White Huns or Hepthalites.

King Skanda Gupta drove back an attempted invasion in 455 CE, but the White Huns continued raiding what is now Pakistan and northwestern India. Their attacks contributed to the collapse of the Gupta Empire, which fragmented into many small states. The White Huns then took advantage of the lack of central control to mount deeper incursions. Under their leaders, Toramana and Mihirakula, the White Huns made their capital at Sakala (modern Sialkot, Pakistan). Chronicle accounts identify Mihirakula as a self-proclaimed worshipper of Shiva and a violent enemy of

These three gold coins are dinars, the currency used in India during the Gupta period.

Adherents of Mahayana and Tantric Buddhism, the Pala were responsible for the introduction of Buddhism in Tibet. In northwestern India, the Rajputs (interrelated clans of fearsome warriors ruled by a military aristocracy) established powerful kingdoms in the 9th, 10th, and 11th centuries CE.

Kings of southern India

In India, the north-south divide is generally taken to be the Vindhya Range, a broken series of hills, around 675 miles (1,086 km) long, that bisects the country. To the south of the range lies the Deccan Plateau; to the north of the range are the vast northern plains of the Ganges and Indus rivers. Southern India was briefly united in the third century BCE under the Mauryan rulers, but its two principal regions developed separately after the death of the last Mauryan emperor, Ashoka, in 233 BCE.

Buddhism; he reputedly destroyed many Buddhist monasteries and temples. After the end of the sixth century CE, the White Huns seem to have disappeared. It is possible that they were driven out of India, but it is more likely that they were assimilated into the local population, as other invaders had been before them.

Regional kingdoms of India

No empire arose to succeed the Guptas in northern India until the Muslim Delhi Sultanate was established in 1206 CE. For more than 600 years, regional kingdoms and republics rose and fell. In the early seventh century CE, King Harsha of Kanauj briefly reunited parts of the Gupta realm from his kingdom north of Delhi, but his empire was short-lived, barely surviving his death.

Meanwhile, in the region of Bengal, the Pala dynasty rose to power around 750 CE and ruled until 1174 CE.

KALIDASA

The poet and dramatist Kalidasa is revered as the greatest writer in Sanskrit. There is some controversy over when he lived, but many historians place his life in the reign of the great Gupta king Chandragupta II (ruled 375–414 CE). Kalidasa's masterpiece is the play *Abhijnanasakuntala* (*Recognition of Sakuntala*), which treats the mythological narrative of the seduction of the nymph Sankantula by King Dushyanta, founder of the Paurav dynasty. The work is celebrated for its lyricism in describing the beauty of nature and the agony of love lost. Kalidasa also wrote two other plays; two epic poems, *Kumarasambhava* (*Birth of the God of War*) and *Raghuvamsa* (*The Dynasty of Raghu*); and a lyric poem, *Meghaduta* (*Messenger of the Clouds*). Kalidasa was probably a priest in the service of Shiva, because his name means "Kali's servant" and the goddess Kali was one of the many forms taken by Shiva's consort, Parvati. The poem *Kumarasambhava* describes the love between Shiva and Parvati and the birth of their son, Kumara, the war god.

The cave complex at Ajanta features 28 rock-cut monuments and 5 monasteries. All were carved out between the second and sixth centuries CE.

SHANKARA AND ADVAITA VEDANTA

Vedanta (meaning "end of the Vedas") was a school of Hindu philosophy that was rooted in statements contained in the Upanishads. Vedanta took several different paths and was formalized in the era of the Guptas and afterward in early medieval India. The great mystic and thinker Shankara, who probably lived in the eighth century CE, was the foremost exponent of the branch known as Advaita Vedanta. Advaita Vedanta proposed that all things were ultimately one, that the *atman* (individual soul) was an aspect of *brahman* (the divine absolute), and that the apparent multiplicity of the universe was, although real, underpinned on a deeper level by unity; it was finally an illusion (*maya* in Sanskrit). The soul was initially prevented by *avidya* (ignorance) from seeing through *maya* and grasping its identity with *brahman*, but through the teachings of the Vedanta, it could do so and thus escape the cycle of birth and death. Other Vedanta teachers included Madhva, who lived in the 13th century CE and taught that the individual soul existed independently of the supreme *brahman*, and Vallabha, who lived in the 15th century CE and placed great emphasis on the grace of a personal god.

The Satavahana kings ruled in southern India from the middle of the third century BCE, first as feudatories of the Mauryan Empire but later independently. They were succeeded by the Pallava dynasty, which also began as subordinate (to the Satavahana kings) but rose to independent power in the fourth century CE with a capital at Kanchi (modern Kanchipuram, in Tamil Nadu).

Among the most notable Pallava kings were Mahendravarman I (ruled 600–630 CE) and his successor, Narasimhavarman I (ruled 630–668 CE). Both kings were great patrons of the arts, especially of rock-cut temples. The beautiful monuments at Mahabalipuram (also known as Mamallapuram) were begun during the reigns of these two kings. The works there include temples, carved reliefs, and a monumental structure named the Five Chariots, in honor of Arjuna, Bhima, Yudhishtra, Nakula, and Sahadeva, the leading Pandava brothers in the epic poem the *Mahabharata*. On December 26, 2004 CE, the catastrophic tsunami (tidal wave) unleashed by an earthquake under the bed of the Indian Ocean uncovered parts of what appear to be an ancient city and temple near Mahabalipuram. As the waters receded with enormous force, they pulled back sand that had covered the buildings for centuries. Underwater excavations by the Archaeological Survey of India were stepped up. Local legends support the theory that these may be part of a large Pallava coastal settlement. According to one story, there was once a large city so beautiful that the gods grew jealous and sent a great flood to conceal its glory.

The Pallavas ruled until the end of the ninth century CE, when their former vassals—the Tamil dynasty of the Cholas—destroyed their power base. The Cholas, in turn, founded an empire that comprised all of southern India and Ceylon (Sri Lanka). At times, their armies advanced as far north as the Ganges River. In the early 11th century CE, the

The temple to Vishnu in Deogarh, Uttar Pradesh, was built in the fifth century CE.

Chola navy under King Rajendra I was the largest ever to sail the Indian Ocean; Rajendra even sponsored a great expedition to the Indonesian archipelago and into Malaysia.

The Chola kings were also great patrons of the arts. Under their rule, superb bronze sculptures were made and large "temple cities" were erected in which the central shrine was surrounded by a multitude of subsidiary shrines, as well as administrative buildings and housing, places for ritual bathing, and even shopping areas. One magnificent example of Chola-period architecture is the Brihadishvara Temple at Tanjore (Thanjavur) in Tamil Nadu. The temple was built between 1003 and 1010 CE by Rajaraja I, founder of the Chola dynasty, in honor of the god Shiva. Its main sanctuary, which contains a simple Shiva *lingam* (phallic post), stands beneath a tower that is 220 feet (67 m) tall and within a courtyard measuring 500 feet by 250 feet (152 m by 76 m). The complex is known to have employed more than 400 dancing girls, hundreds of priests, and no fewer than 50 musicians, as well as gardeners, flower gatherers, makers of garlands, cooks, sculptors, painters, and poets.

The Chola were eventually toppled in the 13th century CE by another Tamil dynasty, the Pandyas. Under Jatavarman Sundara Pandyan (ruled 1251–1268 CE), the Pandya realm expanded as far north as the Krishna River and as far south as Ceylon. However, the power of the Pandyas was ultimately insufficient to withstand the southward expansion of Arab armies in India, and their rule was eclipsed in the 14th century CE by the forces of Islam.

This bronze statuette from the 11th century CE depicts Nataraja (the King of Dance), a manifestation of Shiva, the Hindu god of creation and destruction.

The Chalukya kings

On the Deccan Plateau, the kings of the Chalukya dynasty established themselves in the seventh century CE. The dynasty was founded by Pulakesin I (ruled 543–566 CE), who created a great kingdom in the western Deccan Plateau. His capital was at Badami (in the modern state of Karnataka). The dynasty's foremost ruler was Pulakesin II (ruled 610–642 CE), who expanded the borders of the empire in all directions to take in most of the plateau.

After Pulakesin II died, an eastern branch of the family under his brother, Kubja Vishnuvardhana, set up an independent kingdom that ruled from Vengi until the 11th century CE. Pulakesin II's own branch of the dynasty, the Badami Chalukyas, was eclipsed by the rival Rasthrakuta dynasty, but Chalukya power was restored by the Western Chalyukas, who ruled from Kalyani (modern Basavakalyan in Karnataka) from the 10th century to the 12th century CE.

Muslims in India

The first contact between Islam and India came in the seventh century CE, through Arab traders whose ships landed on the west coast of the country. Relations between visitors and locals were peaceful at first, with some Arabs marrying into local Rajput families. However, in 711 CE, the plundering of Arab ships by Indian pirates led the Umayyad governor of Iraq to launch an attack under Muhammad ibn Qasim. Arab troops conquered Sind, a region of modern Pakistan, and the conquered people converted to Islam.

EXPORT OF INDIAN RELIGIONS

For centuries, the emissaries of Indian princes traveled all over the known world to establish new relationships and to spread the doctrines of their religions. The emissaries sailed to Java, Sumatra, Bali, and Borneo, for example, spreading both Hinduism and Buddhism. The Buddhist temple complex of Borobudur, established in the ninth century CE on the island of Java, is impressive testimony to their evangelical efforts; on the island of Bali in Indonesia, the chief religion is a form of the old Vedic religion with traces of ancient Hinduism. The emissaries also traveled to Cambodia, Burma (Myanmar), and China. In the city of Tamralipti, at the mouth of the Ganges River, ships took on monks as well as cargo. Chinese scholar and pilgrim Yijing (I-tsing), who journeyed to India by way of the Silk Road in 671–695 CE, wrote: "More than a thousand Buddhist monks have applied themselves in the service of scholarship and good works. They investigate and discuss all matters, as they do in India."

Hinduism spread first to southern India, where this temple, the Brihadishvara Temple, was built in the 11th century CE.

Three centuries then passed without further Islamic incursions into India. Then, the Afghan ruler Mahmud of Ghazni launched a series of raids in the 11th century CE. Descended from Turkish and central Asian nomads who had been driven into Persia and Afghanistan by the western expansion of China, Mahmud made at least 17 annual expeditions into India from his capital at Ghazni in eastern Afghanistan.

On one of these raids, in 1024 CE, Mahmud of Ghazni led his troops to the great Hindu temple of Shiva at Somnath, near Veraval in western Gujarat. A large gilded *lingam* was worshipped there. According to an Arab source from the 13th century CE, the *lingam* was washed daily with water from the Ganges River. More than 1,000 water carriers brought the water every day, and the temple employed 1,000 priests and 600 musicians, dancers, and servants. Mahmud attacked and looted the temple, personally smashing the *lingam* with a hammer. More than 50,000 Indians died trying to defend the temple. According to tradition, the temple destroyed by Mahmud was the third

When Mahmud of Ghazni died around 1030 CE, he was buried in this mausoleum at Ghazni, Afghanistan.

such structure on the site. Little is known of the first temple, but the second was destroyed by Junayad, the Arab ruler of Sind, in 725 CE and then rebuilt. After the attack of 1024 CE, the Somnath temple was destroyed by Muslims on three further occasions—in 1297 CE, 1394 CE, and 1706 CE—and rebuilt each time. The latest reconstruction was completed in 1995 CE.

Mahmud did not establish a lasting presence in India. Although his territory nominally extended from Persia to the Ganges River, in practice, his power in India was restricted to the northern frontier regions, and even there, it was effective only during his annual expeditions.

The Delhi Sultanate

The first Muslim empire in India was the Delhi Sultanate, which was made possible by the capture of Delhi in 1192 CE by another Afghan ruler, Muhammad of Ghur. The sultanate was ruled by a succession of Turko-Afghan dynasties (see box, page 970), beginning in 1206 CE, when Muhammad of Ghur was assassinated and his general Qutb-ud-

Local people carry goods across the sand to the Hindu temple of Shiva on the seashore at Somnath, in Gujarat, India.

Din Aybak took power, proclaiming himself the sultan of Delhi. Qutb-ud-Din Aybak built the Qutb Minar—a brick tower 240 feet (73 m) tall—as a symbol of Muslim victory in India and established the dynasty of the Mamluks. The Mamluk (Slave) dynasty, which lasted until 1290 CE, derived its name from the fact that many of the rulers were slaves or children of slaves who had converted to Islam and won glory as soldiers, thereby raising their social status.

Most subjects of the Delhi sultans were Hindus who were unwilling to accept Muslim rule. Time and again, the Islamic rulers faced uprisings. Only in regions where the Muslims had garrisons and fortifications was there any measure of stability.

The Delhi Sultanate reached its greatest extent around 1330 CE. At that point, Sultan Muhammad ibn Tughluq (ruled 1325–1351 CE) attempted to move the capital from Delhi to Daulatabad, a city on the Deccan Plateau from which Muhammad thought he would be able to exert more effective control over the southern provinces. However, his attempts to forge a unified empire failed as provincial governors and nobles rebelled and set up their own independent sultanates, such as the Shahi dynasty in Bengal, which declared independence from Delhi in 1338 CE.

The power of the Tughluq dynasty was severely and lastingly damaged in 1398 CE, when Tamerlane (Timur the Lame), the Mongol ruler of Samarkand, launched a devastating raid on Delhi. In the wake of the Mongol attack, the Tughluq sultans controlled little more than the city of Delhi and its immediate vicinity. Although the sultanate later recovered some of its former territories, the rulers generally resigned themselves to the fact that their rule in India was now no more than nominal.

THE DYNASTIES OF THE DELHI SULTANATE

The Delhi Sultanate lasted from 1206 to 1526 CE, when it was eclipsed by the rise of the Mughal dynasty. A succession of Turkish and Afghan families ruled from Delhi during those 320 years.

The first dynasty was that of the Mamluks, established by Qutb-ud-Din Aybak, a Turkish ex-slave who had been the general of Afghan ruler Muhammad of Ghur. The Mamluks ruled until 1290 CE, when they were replaced by another Afghan dynasty, that of the Khalji, founded by Jalal-ud-Din Firuz. Jalal's son, Ala-ud-Din Khalji, repelled a number of attempted Mongol invasions.

The Khalji dynasty was succeeded by the Turkish Tughluq family, which ruled until 1413 CE. The Tughluq dynasty was founded by Ghazi Malik, who ruled as Ghiyath-al-Din Tughluq. The Sayyid dynasty (ruled 1414–1451 CE) rose to power during the period of lawlessness that followed the decline of Tughluq authority after the sack of Delhi by Tamerlane (Timur the Lame) in 1398 CE. The Sayyid dynasty was founded by Khizr Khan.

The rule of the final dynasty of the Delhi Sultanate, the Afghan Lodhi dynasty, began when a military governor in Punjab named Bahlul Khan Lodhi seized the throne in Delhi in 1451 CE. He and his descendants ruled for 75 years but lost power when they were defeated at the Battle of Panipat in 1526 CE by the Afghan ruler Babur, who founded the Mughal Empire.

The Delhi Sultanate came to an end in April of 1526 CE, when Ibrahim Lodhi, the third ruler of the Lodhi dynasty, was defeated near Panipat, north of Delhi, by the Afghan ruler Babur, a descendant of Tamerlane and Genghis Khan. Babur conquered large areas of India and founded the Mughal dynasty that would rule much of India until the middle of the 18th century CE.

The Qutb Minar was built near Delhi in the 13th century CE by Muslim rulers of northern India.

Developments in the south

On the Deccan Plateau, the Bahmani Sultanate was established in 1347 CE, when the Turkish governor Ala-ud-Din Bahman Shah rebelled against the Tughluq sultan in Delhi, Muhammad ibn Tughluq. Ala-ud-Din Bahman Shah established a capital at Ahsanabad (modern Gulbarga, in the state of Karnataka). Farther south, the Hindu kingdom of Vijayanagar was established in 1336 CE by Harihara Raya I and his brother, Bukka Raya I. At its height, their empire comprised all of India to the south of the Krishna River. Their capital, Vijayanagar (City of Victory; modern Hampi in Karnataka), was a vast and hugely wealthy metropolis containing arcade bazaars and stone-cut waterways, with beautiful gardens, a great royal palace, and numerous temples. Vijayanagar won fame around the world on the basis of reports from traders and travelers; in 1522 CE, a Portuguese adventurer named Paes reported that it was "as large as Rome" and "the best-provided of the world's cities." Today, the ruins of Vijayanagar cover an area of 15 square miles (40 km^2).

Around 1400 CE, the Bahmani Sultanate divided into five states: Bijapur, Golconda, Ahmadnagar, Bidar, and Berar. The five states waged separate wars with Vijayanagar until 1564 CE, when they allied to win a decisive victory over the Hindu kingdom. The City of Victory was abandoned forever. However, although the kingdoms of the Deccan Plateau were successful in their war in the south, they were exhausted by the struggle, and their resources were depleted. Their weakness paved the way for their defeat and absorption into the Mughal Empire (including Golconda in 1687 CE).

The age of the sultans had a great influence on Indian society. Muslims and Hindus associated with each other to a certain extent, while some of the sultanate rulers exercised a degree of tolerance toward Islam's rival religions. Sanskrit lost its position as the official language of the country, enabling a number of the regional Indian languages to achieve independent prominence.

This 16th-century-CE painting depicts Babur, the founder of the Mughal Empire.

See also:

India's First Civilizations (volume 7, page 918) • The Mongols (volume 9, page 1218)

SOUTHEAST ASIA

The peoples of Southeast Asia were strongly linked in prehistory, but by the end of the first millennium of the Common Era, they had developed along divergent paths. A number of trading empires flourished between the 13th and 15th centuries CE.

The earliest known human inhabitants of Southeast Asia lived around 40,000 years ago. At that time, the whole region was one extensive landmass; the seas that now separate the Indochina Peninsula (Cambodia, Laos, Myanmar, Thailand, and Vietnam) from Island Southeast Asia (Indonesia and the Philippines) appeared when global water levels rose by around 150 feet (50 m) between 7000 and 6000 BCE. The comparatively young topography of the region helps to explain why many areas of Southeast Asia have more in common culturally and traditionally than their apparent modern isolation might suggest.

A good illustration of the continuity of early civilization across the region may be seen in the archaeological remnants of the Hoabinhian Age (c. 13,000–4000 BCE). First identified in Vietnam, stone tools of similar design were later excavated in Cambodia, Laos, Myanmar, Sumatra, and Thailand. Some researchers believe that Hoabinhian influence extended as far as southern China, Nepal, Taiwan, and even Australia.

By around 3000 BCE, the rise in sea level had inspired generations of mariners, who traded, settled, and spread their languages across half the world south of the equator. Southeast Asia's earliest sailors ventured out from Taiwan to Indonesia, Java, the Philippines, and various islands of the Pacific and Indian oceans, where their Proto-Austronesian tongues developed into modern Malayo-Polynesian languages. Today, languages of this group are spoken across the region from Madagascar in the west, through New Zealand and Polynesia, to Hawaii in the east.

Southeast Asia had two other main language groups. One was Tibeto-Burman, which was spoken by Himalayan mountain peoples who moved to lower ground in the eighth century BCE and settled along the Irrawaddy River. Tibeto-Burman developed into Burmese, the language of modern Myanmar. The other language group was Austroasiatic, from which developed modern Khmer, Lao, Thai, and Vietnamese.

Dong Son

The gradual disconnection of the Indochina Peninsula from developments in Island Southeast Asia is reflected in the increasingly separate evolution of agriculture and metallurgy. By around 2000 BCE, the inhabitants of northeastern Thailand and northern Vietnam were

This relief sculpture depicting a dancer decorates the walls of the Bayon Temple in present-day Cambodia. The temple was built around 1300 CE.

SOUTHEAST ASIA

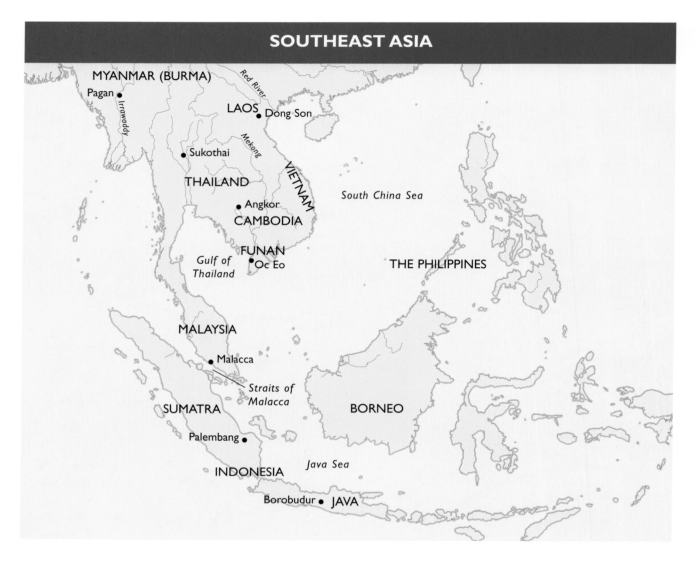

employing methods of cultivating rice and making bronze that were quite unlike those used in the islands and even in neighboring China and India. During the next thousand years, increasingly sophisticated metalworking techniques emerged in the Indochina Peninsula. The artifacts discovered at a settlement in northern Vietnam show how far metallurgy had advanced by around 1000 BCE. The village in question, Dong Son, has given its name to the whole civilization of the period. The earliest artifacts found there are plowshares, axes, sickles, spearheads, fishhooks, and various items of jewelry. By around 500 BCE, the Dong Son were producing bronze drums that weighed more than 150 pounds (68 kg) and were decorated with geometric shapes and depictions of animals and humans. The similarities between their great stone monuments and those found in the distant islands of Polynesia suggest that the Dong Son were seafarers.

The Dong Son cultivated rice, which had already become the staple diet of the greater part of Southeast Asia. The crop was grown mainly in the fertile plains of the main rivers—notably the Irrawaddy, the Mekong, and the Red—and it was there that the greatest concentrations of population emerged. The upland and mountain areas became—and remain—sparsely populated.

The other main crop was the sago palm, which formed the basis of the diet for people living in eastern Indonesia. The people of Southeast Asia as a whole did not traditionally raise herds of animals, such as cattle or pigs. Much of their protein came from fish, which were farmed in rice fields and ponds. People living near lakes and rivers developed bamboo traps to catch fish, and fishing was the foremost occupation along the coasts.

Chinese and Indian influence

Shortly before the beginning of the Common Era, Southeast Asia came under the influence of its neighbors, India to the west and China to the north. In the late second century BCE, Chinese peoples subjugated northern Vietnam. The conquered region, Annam, remained a distant outpost of the Chinese Empire for more than a thousand years, despite constant opposition from the Vietnamese. The Chinese introduced their own government and their Confucian, Taoist, and Buddhist religions. Buddhism, in particular, became highly influential throughout Southeast Asia.

India's influence was more subtle. There is no evidence of any Indian invasion of Southeast Asia, but by around 500 CE, Indochinese sculptors were carving statues of Vishnu, an important god in the Indian Hindu religion. Inscriptions in Sanskrit started to appear on ornamental stones erected in several parts of Southeast Asia, including Vietnam, Malaysia, Borneo, and Java. Sanskrit was a ritual language that was not spoken in everyday life; it was used only by Indian priests and scholars. Everyday Indian languages, such as Tamil, had little influence on Southeast Asia, suggesting that few Indians themselves traveled to the region. The implication is that the cul-

ture of Southeast Asia came under relatively little external pressure, and when it did, it was strong enough to assimilate exotic influences rather than be subsumed by them.

Mandalas

The earliest known Southeast Asian kingdom is Funan, which was located near the southern tip of modern Vietnam. Records of Funan are sketchy, and the only firm evidence of its existence is in the records of Chinese envoys, who made an inward mission there in the third century CE to investigate its thriving sea trade. Chinese diplomatic records are also the main source of modern knowledge about other important trading kingdoms that sprang up later in the Malay Peninsula and on the islands of Sumatra and Java.

However, while kingdoms became the norm in Europe, they remained

This bronze drum was made by people of the Dong Son culture between the third century and the first century BCE.

This stone statue of the Hindu god Ganesh was made in Thailand in the 10th century CE.

until the height of European colonialism in the 19th century CE.

No two mandalas were alike; the unique structure of each was determined by its location and economy. Some of the best-documented sites were along the coast of central Vietnam, in the Mekong River Delta, in the valleys of the Chao Phraya and Irrawaddy rivers, and on the islands of Borneo and Java.

Two great empires

One of the most prosperous and enduring mandalas was Srivijaya (a name meaning "Glorious Victory"), whose capital was located near Palembang, in southern Sumatra. By the late seventh century CE, Srivijaya controlled the Straits of Malacca, the strategically important channel linking the Indian Ocean with the South China and Java seas. During the next 400 years, Srivijaya became wealthy by trading and by taxing cargo ships that passed through the straits.

The mercantile empire of Srivijaya reflected Southeast Asia's long maritime history. Sailors in prehistoric times had reached as far as the east coast of Africa. Later, Chinese sources listed Southeast Asians among the most important trading groups that were allowed to reside in ports on China's southern coast.

unusual in Southeast Asia, mainly because the region's contact with India had inspired a lasting political change—the adoption of mandalas. A mandala is effectively equivalent to a modern state but is defined by spheres of influence rather than by geographical frontiers. Mandalas remained the predominant form of government in Southeast Asia

Perhaps even greater than the achievements of Srivijaya were those of the Khmer (Cambodian) state that flourished in the Tonle Sap (Great Lake) region between the 9th and 13th centuries CE. The prosperity of the Khmers was derived from a highly advanced system of water collection and dispersal that facilitated the production of four rice crops a year. The Khmer civilization was fundamentally a mandala, but it grew into an empire with full imperial trappings, including a state deity—*devaraja* (meaning "a god who is king")—and numerous monumental buildings.

The greatest of these buildings to survive is Angkor Wat, a temple that was built between around 1100 and 1150 CE and dedicated to Vishnu. Angkor Wat was constructed on the orders of the Khmer king Suryavarman II, who may have intended the gigantic structure to house his body after his death. The temple's five towers represent the five peaks of Mount Meru (home of the Hindu gods), while the moat around the complex represents the oceans that surround Meru in Hindu mythology. Despite its Hindu origins, Angkor Wat was later used as a Buddhist temple. Now a UNESCO World Heritage Site, the temple has become a symbol of Cambodia, even appearing on the national flag.

The golden age

The problem with the early Khmer society was that it sacrificed the adaptability of the mandala for the less flexible structure of the Western-style state. Thus, when surrounding mandalas suffered periods of adversity, it was unable to compensate for their shortcomings. When the Khmer state fell on hard times, it could not recover; by around 1300 CE, it had virtually disintegrated. At around the same time, Srivijaya fell to the Majapahit, an Indianized Hindu empire that came to dominate the region.

The end of the two greatest civilizations of Southeast Asia might have been expected to usher in a period of uncertainty and even anarchy. However, on the contrary, the 14th century CE witnessed the dawn of a golden age that lasted until the coming of European colonists almost 500 years later.

The success was attributable to numerous factors, including the willingness of each regional culture to assimilate and coexist with exotic economic, political, and religious influences, rather than oppose them. Also significant was the entrepreneurial spirit of the Southeast Asian peoples, who proved remarkably adaptable to changing methods of trade.

The period saw the emergence of five main regional powers: the Ava, who ruled Burma (Myanmar) from 1364 to 1752 CE; the Later Le dynasty, which governed Vietnam from 1428 to 1788 CE; the Ayutthaya, who controlled much of Thailand from 1351 to 1767 CE; the Malacca, who flourished in the Malay Peninsula from 1400 to 1511 CE; and the Majapahit, who, having defeated the Srivijaya mandala, controlled Java until around 1527 CE.

Those major potentates did not always coexist peacefully, and from time to time, they also came into conflict with some of the numerous smaller states that also prospered in the region, including Chiang Mai, part of modern Thailand. In mainland Southeast Asia, several peoples vied for power. While northern Vietnam was controlled by the Dai Viet dynasty, southern Vietnam was ruled by the

This gargoyle, known as a Kirtimukha, was made by the inhabitants of Oc Eo, a port that flourished in Vietnam between the first and seventh centuries CE.

Austronesian-speaking Cham people. The Cham, accomplished carvers and temple-builders, were subdued by the Vietnamese in the 15th century CE. In Thailand and southern Burma, meanwhile, the Austroasiatic Mon people were important traders and rulers. The Mon were eventually defeated by two other peoples. In the west, they fell to the Burmese, who established a great Buddhist kingdom called Pagan during the 11th century CE. In present-day Thailand, the Mon were defeated by the Thai, who established their own capital at Sukothai in the 13th century CE. However, the period as a whole was characterized by vigorous trade rather than by warfare. There was profitable traffic across Southeast Asia in a wide range of goods, from ceramics, metals, and precious gemstones to salted dried fish and rice.

The five towers of Angkor Wat, a Khmer temple located in present-day Cambodia, represent the five peaks of Mount Meru, home of the Hindu gods.

Economic prosperity fueled an artistic and cultural renaissance, during which the various civilizations strove to mark out their own identities. That desire was perhaps strongest in northern Vietnam, where the inhabitants were anxious to establish their independence from the Chinese who had dominated them for nearly a thousand years. In Java and Burma, the Sanskrit inscriptions stopped at the end of the 13th century CE. Thereafter, the culture of both places became identifiably national—Javanese and Burmese, respectively.

Urbanization and Europeans

The 13th century CE brought an influx of Chinese immigrants to Southeast Asia. The newcomers provided an important stimulus to the growth of cities in the region. Most Southeast Asian capitals, such as Angkor, were still mainly

THE IMPORTANCE OF RELIGION

After Southeast Asia fell under the influence of India and China, Hinduism and, later, Buddhism, became the region's dominant religions. The region's native religions probably involved ancestor worship, with rituals to ask the spirits of the dead to protect the living. Such beliefs survive today among some of the hill tribes in remote areas. Elsewhere, too, Hindu ideas did not replace earlier beliefs. Instead, Southeast Asians used Indian religious symbols to express their own ideas in a more complex way. In Java, for example, many early Hindu temples were built on high mountains, in places where the Javanese traditionally believed that the spirits of their ancestors dwelled.

Another development that came from Southeast Asia rather than from India was the claim of some rulers to be gods themselves. The practice began in the Cambodian kingdom of Angkor in the 10th century CE. A usurper, Jayavarman IV, established the legitimacy of his kingship by claiming to be an incarnation of Shiva. Claims grew ever more extravagant until the early 13th century CE, when Jayavarman VII boasted that he was greater than all the Hindu gods combined.

In Indonesia, Buddhist rulers attempted to portray themselves as *bodhisattvas*, holy beings who had reached a state of divine enlightenment but remained in existence in order to help other beings attain enlightenment too. As in Cambodia, the tendency began slowly but gradually grew more exaggerated.

Southeast Asians were generally tolerant of rival religions. In many places, Hinduism and Buddhism coexisted peacefully. One ninth-century-CE Javanese king married a Buddhist queen, and together the couple built both Buddhist and Hindu temples. The Buddhist shrine Borobudur, built around 800 CE, is one of the largest Buddhist edifices in the world, but many Hindu sites are found nearby, suggesting the peaceful coexistence of the two beliefs. In the Majapahit period that began in Java at the end of the 13th century CE, several rulers were worshipped in the form of statues of both Hindu and Buddhist deities. The last great monument built at Angkor, the Khmer capital, was Buddhist. The preceding Hindu monuments were left as they were and often simply taken over for Buddhist worship.

This bronze sculpture depicts the head of the Khmer king Jayavarman VII, a Buddhist who was believed to have reached a divine state.

The Dhammayangyi Temple was built in the ancient kingdom of Pagan, now part of present-day Myanmar.

religious and ceremonial centers, with relatively few inhabitants and strictly limited economic activity. Beginning in the 13th century CE, however, and accelerating into the 14th century CE, cities in the modern sense began to form in several coastal areas of Southeast Asia.

Malacca, for example, founded on the Malay Peninsula in 1400 CE, was a thriving port. The imperial Chinese fleet docked in the city's harbor on seven occasions between 1403 and 1433 CE. At the time, the natives welcomed the opportunity for trade, but foreign interest in the region would later increase with severely damaging effects.

The Chinese, stung by their defeat by the Vietnamese in 1427 CE, renounced any expansionist ambitions in Southeast Asia. The Europeans, however, had suffered no such adverse experiences, and after the entry of the Portuguese into Malacca in 1509 CE, Westerners soon became the most destructive interlopers

of all. At first, their visits aroused little local comment. Long-distance sea voyages were already unremarkable, and Asia had had limited but steady contact with the West since the time of Marco Polo (c. 1254–1324 CE). The Southeast Asians again welcomed the economic benefits of foreign visits, but the Europeans cast covetous eyes on the wealth of the region and sought ways to exploit it.

Spice wealth

As early as imperial Roman times, Europeans had been eager to import spices from the East. The most important such products grew in Indonesia. Pepper was found in many of Indonesia's 18,000 islands, while nutmeg and cloves grew in only one small area—the Spice Islands, now called the Moluccas, which lay in northeastern Indonesia.

The quest for spices lay behind much of the European expansion that occurred in the 16th century CE. The explorer

Christopher Columbus was hoping to find a route to the Spice Islands when he landed in the Americas in 1492 CE. The European demand for spices to flavor food could yield considerable riches for those who were prepared to travel to search for them.

At this time, only the Spanish in the Philippines had colonial ambitions; the aim elsewhere was simply to take as much as possible at the least expense. The Portuguese capture of Malacca in 1511 CE began a new and inauspicious chapter in Southeast Asian history, which reached its lowest point in the 19th century CE, when Britain, France, and Portugal took parts of Southeast Asia into their empires.

Regional religion

The period immediately prior to the start of European incursions into Southeast Asia was a time of great religious upheaval. On the mainland, both Hinduism (which was dominant in Cambodia) and Mahayana Buddhism (which had been popular among the Mon) gave way to Theravada Buddhism, a belief system that was simpler but more exclusive than its predecessor.

The island region, meanwhile, saw the introduction of Islam from Arabia. Islam gained a foothold in Sumatra in the late 13th century CE; some Malays and Javanese later converted. In the 15th century CE, Malacca became the first major kingdom to adopt Islam. Through Malacca's commercial connections, Islam spread to most of the rest of the archipelago along trade routes. For the first European arrivals in Indonesia, at least one aspect of life was familiar; the struggle between Christendom and Islam had a new battlefield.

See also:

The Buddha and Buddhism (volume 7, page 946) • European Expansion (volume 10, page 1360) • Hinduism: The Religion of India (volume 7, page 932)

The Kampung Kling Mosque is located in Malacca, a state in present-day Malaysia. Malacca has been a Muslim state since the 15th century CE.

CULTURES OF THE PACIFIC

The first civilizations on the islands of the Pacific Ocean emerged around 30,000 years ago. Some of the cultures that developed on these islands remained isolated from the rest of the world until as late as the 18th century CE.

TIME LINE

c. 30,000 BCE
Lapita culture develops in New Guinea.

c. 1000 BCE
Lapita culture reaches Fiji.

c. 100 CE
Inhabitants of Indonesia begin to migrate eastward and settle in Micronesia and Polynesia.

c. 400 CE
First settlers arrive on Easter Island.

1520 CE
Portuguese explorer Ferdinand Magellan becomes first European to enter Pacific Ocean.

1642 CE
Abel Tasman sights New Zealand.

1722 CE
Jacob Roggeveen discovers Easter Island, so named because he arrived there on Easter Sunday.

1769 CE
James Cook arrives in Tahiti.

There are approximately 25,000 islands scattered over an area of around 64 million square miles (165 million km²) in the Pacific Ocean. Some of these islands are clustered together in groups; others are among the most remote places on earth. None is more cut off than Easter Island (see box, page 986), which is 1,200 miles (1,900 km) east of its closest neighbor, Pitcairn Island, and 2,200 miles (3,500 km) from the coast of Chile in South America.

The three Pacific island groups

The islands of the Pacific are conventionally categorized into three large groups: Melanesia, Micronesia, and Polynesia. Melanesia (from the Greek *melas*, meaning "black," and *nesos*, meaning "island") is named for the predominantly dark-skinned peoples who originally inhabited New Guinea (the largest Pacific island), the Bismarck Archipelago, Fiji, Vanuatu, New Caledonia, and the Solomon Islands.

Micronesia (from the Greek for "small islands") lies mainly to the north of the equator and to the east of the Philippines. (The Philippines, although themselves a collection of islands in the Pacific Ocean, are generally treated separately from the three main groups under consideration here.) Micronesia consists of around 2,000 islands, the largest and most important of which are the Northern Marianas, Palau (Belau), the Marshall Islands, Tuvalu, Kiribati, Nauru, and the Federated States of Micronesia (a republic that incorporates the Caroline Islands and has its capital at Palikir on Pohnpei Island). The smallest landfalls in Micronesia are no more than coral atolls (reefs), most of which are uninhabited.

The main islands of Polynesia (from the Greek for "many islands") are the Hawaiian Islands, New Zealand, and Easter Island. Within the triangle that they form are Samoa, Tahiti, Tonga, the Society Islands, the Tuamotu Archipelago, the Marquesas Islands, and the Cook Islands.

The islands of the Pacific Ocean are so far apart and so different in character that it is difficult to make generalizations that hold for all—or even most—of them. Another problem facing people who wish to study their cultures is that of accurate historical documentation. The islands were unknown to Europeans until the 16th century CE. Many of the indigenous peoples have their own records of ancient times, but their accounts—based mainly on oral tradition—are not necessarily historically

This wooden sculpture, dating to the 17th or 18th century CE, depicts the Polynesian creator god, Tangaroa.

982

ISLANDS OF THE PACIFIC

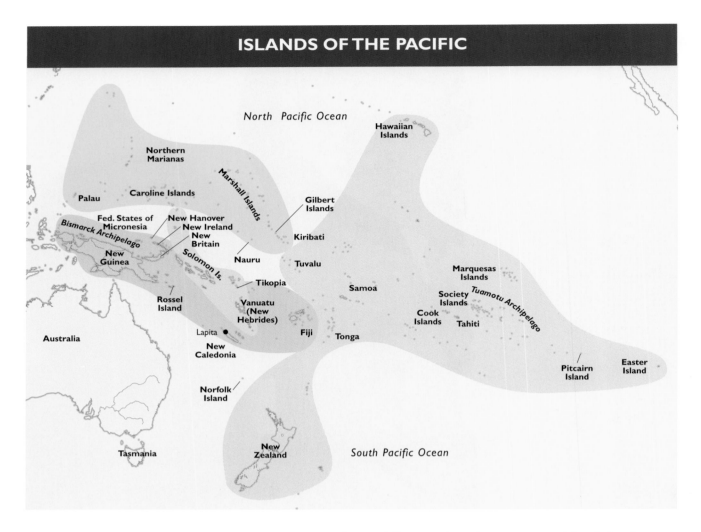

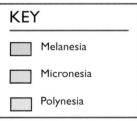

KEY

- Melanesia
- Micronesia
- Polynesia

accurate, and they are not always fully understood by modern scholars.

Early settlements

The first confirmed civilization in the Pacific arose around 30,000 BCE. Although it is known as the Lapita culture (from the site in New Caledonia where the earliest relics were unearthed in the 20th century CE), it is thought to have originated in New Guinea, which was still joined to Australia at the time. (The two lands were later divided by sea around 10,000 years ago.) Lapita pottery reached Tasmania by around 9000 BCE and Fiji by around 1000 BCE. It was then transported by sea to Tonga, Samoa, and Micronesia. The Lapita culture had spread to eastern Polynesia by 500 BCE

and to the Marquesas Islands by the second century BCE.

The pioneer migrants to the most distant parts of the Pacific are thought to have originally been Indonesians who were displaced by settlers from continental Asia. The eastward migration left traces as far as Polynesia, but the only permanent settlements were in Micronesia. In all other areas, the early settlers were either driven out or exterminated by later waves of immigrants. It is assumed that the people who migrated between 100 and 1000 CE followed two routes: a southern path through New Guinea and Samoa to the archipelagoes of the central Pacific and a northern path through the Caroline and Marshall islands to the farthest reaches of

Polynesia. The edges of Polynesia were the last parts of the region to be inhabited. Easter Island was reached around 400 CE, while New Zealand and the Hawaiian Islands were first settled between around 750 and 1000 CE.

Thereafter, technological development was slow throughout the region. The main reasons for that are clear; most of the islands were too far apart for the dissemination and cross-fertilization of ideas. Also, competition was minimal; despite the limited resources available to them, each society was self-sufficient. Even on individual islands, coastal communities were often cut off from each other by impassable mountainous interiors; that was particularly true of New Guinea but also applied to smaller islands, such as the Hawaiian Islands, Samoa, and the Society Islands—which are all steep volcanic protrusions rising out of the sea.

It was a consequence of these limitations that, by the time the first Europeans

OCEANGOING CANOES

Contact between the various Pacific island groups may have been limited, but it was not nonexistent. The most wide-ranging islanders were the Polynesians, who could, on occasion, cover distances of more than 5,000 miles (8,000 km). They undertook such journeys in canoes, some up to 100 feet (30 m) long, made from hollowed-out tree trunks. For the longer expeditions, they used a double boat—a large canoe for the rowers and a small one for the provisions, with the two vessels being joined by a wooden bridge.

The rations on board were mainly breadfruit, which could stay fresh for more than a year, and coconuts, which provided both food and drink. Water was stored in bamboo casks. The Polynesians navigated by the stars, but they were also familiar with prevailing winds and ocean currents. Some kept charts of ocean currents drawn on pieces of wood.

Pola Island is part of American Samoa, one of the island groupings that make up Polynesia.

EASTER ISLAND

The first European to sight Easter Island was the Dutchman Jacob Roggeveen, who spent a single day—Easter Sunday—there in 1722 CE. In 1770 CE, the island was found again by a Spanish expedition from Peru. Four years later, James Cook "discovered" it once more. When French navigator Jean-François de Galaup landed there in 1786 CE, he became the fourth European to think that he was the first Westerner to see it.

Easter Island is famous for the gigantic stone statues—more than 600 of them—that decorate the coast and the slopes of the extinct central volcano, Rano Raraku. The statues are human effigies and have stone platforms (*ahus*) on their landward sides. The oldest of them were erected between 700 and 850 CE.

There are no similar statues anywhere else in Polynesia, although there are some similarities between them and Aztec megaliths in Central America. Each statue stands between 10 and 20 feet (3–6 m) tall and weighs between 25 and 82 tons (25.4–83.3 metric tonnes). The indigenous peoples had no lifting apparatus and seemed, like all the other inhabitants of Polynesia, to be technologically primitive. Therefore, the Europeans were soon preoccupied with how the statues had been put into position.

The lack of firm evidence about the origin of the statues inspired numerous theories, some plausible, others preposterous. One of the most famously far-fetched theories was that of Swiss author Erich von Däniken, whose *Chariots of the Gods* proposed that the statues were installed by extraterrestrials. The book, published in 1968 CE, was an international best-seller. What it failed to take into account, however, was that reenactments carried out more than a decade earlier had demonstrated that the Easter Islanders were easily capable of moving the great carvings themselves.

This ancient stone statue is just one of several hundred on Easter Island.

arrived by ship, the societies of the Pacific Ocean were still Neolithic in character. The inhabitants' tools were made of stone, bone, and shell. Almost the only edible native plants were bananas, breadfruit, calabash (bottle gourds), coconuts, pineapples, taro, and yams. The one vegetable import of exotic origin was the sweet potato, which had been brought to Polynesia from South America in prehistory.

The indigenous peoples made cloth from the bark of the Asiatic paper mulberry tree and rope from the bark of the *Triumfetta semitriloba*. They had only three domesticated animals—chickens, dogs, and pigs—which had been imported from Asia. The islanders were skilled at sea fishing and navigation, but they nevertheless had only limited contact with neighboring islands; the distances between each outcrop in the ocean were generally too great to be undertaken in the islanders' tiny sailing vessels. Such subsistence cultures generally had no use for art; Lapita pottery was abandoned in Samoa and the Marquesas Islands shortly after it had been introduced.

People and language

The ancient peoples of Melanesia were enormously diverse. However, some generalizations may safely be made. One is that they were often clearly divided between coastal and inland populations. The former traditionally had the most frequent contact with other islands, while the latter tended to remain isolated from external influences. In both areas, the main occupation was pig farming. Societies were patrilineal; each community had its own "big man," a title that was passed from father to son. Melanesians were animists; they practiced magic and worshiped totems.

In Micronesia, the early populations were concentrated by the seashore (many of the islands are too small to have inte-

This wooden figure of a human was made in Hawaii and dates to the 18th century CE. Hawaiians believed that their gods could be induced to enter figures such as this.

TATTOOING

Tattoos (permanent marks on the skin made by the injection of pigments) were fairly common in Europe before the Common Era, notably in Britain, France, Germany, Greece, and Italy. However, with the spread of Christianity, the practice fell into disuse and was largely forgotten. The church even went so far as to ban tattooing on the basis of Leviticus 19:28 in the Old Testament of the Bible: "You shall not make any cuts in your body for the dead nor make any tattoo marks on yourselves: I am the Lord."

When James Cook visited Tahiti in 1769 CE, he found that tattoos were much in evidence among the indigenous population. The English explorer was particularly fascinated by the multipointed, rakelike instrument used by local tattooists to make the initial incision. His reports back to England revived tattooing there and elsewhere in Europe. The English word *tattoo* comes from the Tahitian language.

This painting from the 16th or 17th century CE depicts the Portuguese explorer Ferdinand Magellan, the first European to sail in the Pacific Ocean.

before the 16th century CE. Polynesians were also the most accomplished of the Pacific peoples at carving wood and stone. Their family structures attached almost equal value to both matriarchal and patriarchal traditions. Polynesian faith was based on *mana*, a spiritual quality that was believed to be invested by supernatural forces in individuals, organizations, and inanimate objects. Although the concept of *mana* was also familiar in Melanesia and Micronesia, it was in Polynesia (particularly among the Maoris of New Zealand) that the belief system was most fully developed.

Around 450 languages are spoken in the Pacific islands. They all belong to the Austronesian family and derive ultimately from Proto-Oceanic, a notional common ancestor that originated in Taiwan. Today, the most common Oceanic languages are Samoan and Eastern Fijian (around 300,000 native speakers each), followed by Kiribati, Kuanua, Maori, and Tongan (around 100,000 each). The total number of speakers of the modern Oceanic languages is thought to be no more than two million, which is probably the highest total in history. Still, that is an average of fewer than 4,500 speakers per language, further testament to the isolation of each small pocket of civilization.

Explorers from the West

The first European to reach Oceania was Ferdinand Magellan (c. 1480–1521 CE), a Portuguese explorer who, having rounded Cape Horn, entered (and named) the Pacific Ocean in 1520 CE. He was followed in 1567 CE by his compatriot, Álvaro de Mendaña de Neira, who visited the Solomon Islands. In 1606 CE, Pedro Fernández de Quirós discovered the Tuamotu Archipelago, the northern Cook Islands, Tikopia, and the New Hebrides (Vanuatu). One of Quirós's shipmates, Luis Váez de Torres,

riors worthy of the name) and worked in fishing or short-haul interisland trade. In contrast to Melanesia, many Micronesian societies were matrilineal; property and honorary titles were passed from generation to generation on the mother's side. Group worship was unusual; most religious observances were conducted privately within families or clans.

Of the early inhabitants of the three main island groups, those of Polynesia are the easiest to summarize. Their main commercial activities were fishing and pig farming. Artistically, they were the most productive of the Pacific islanders, and they accorded their bards and sculptors the same high social recognition as their warriors and civic leaders. Polynesian mythological epics and genealogies are important sources of information about Pacific island life

later reached southeastern New Guinea. Portugal then abandoned exploration of the region because it seemed to offer little or no commercial opportunity.

The next wave of European explorers came from Holland. In 1615–1616 CE, Jakob Le Maire visited Tonga, New Ireland, and New Hanover. In 1642 CE, Abel Tasman sighted New Zealand, Tonga, some of the Fiji Islands, and New Britain. In 1722 CE, while crossing the Pacific Ocean from east to west, Jacob Roggeveen found Easter Island, the northern Society Islands, and some of the Samoan islands. He also rediscovered parts of the Tuamotu Archipelago. The Dutch then lost interest in exploring the region, for much the same reason as the Portuguese had.

The British first arrived in the area in the 18th century CE. In 1700 CE, the pirate William Dampier sailed the Royal Navy ship under his command, HMS *Roebuck*, into New Hanover, New Britain, and New Ireland. In 1765 CE, Admiral John Byron found more of the Tuamotu Archipelago and the southern Gilbert Islands (now part of Kiribati). In 1767 CE, Samuel Wallis found Tahiti, more of the Tuamotu Archipelago, and the Society Islands. In the same year, Philip Carteret found Pitcairn Island and rediscovered the Solomon Islands.

In 1768 CE, French navigator Louis-Antoine de Bougainville sighted some of the New Hebrides and Rossel Island in the Louisiade Archipelago.

The Pacific islands had virtually no exploitable resources and were therefore not really worth colonizing. However, Dampier's and Bougainville's published descriptions of their journeys captured the European imagination and inspired English sea captain James Cook's three voyages to Oceania. Cook first went to Tahiti in 1769 CE, to observe the transit of Venus (when the planet passes between the sun and the earth) and to

search for the legendary—and, as it turned out, mythical—antipodean continent known as Southland. While sailing the South Seas, Cook found previously uncharted islands in the Tuamotu Archipelago, the Marquesas Islands, Fiji, New Caledonia, and the New Hebrides, as well as Norfolk Island and a group known to the Maoris as Kuki Airani but subsequently renamed the Cook Islands in his honor. Cook's final voyage (1776–1779 CE) concentrated on the North Pacific, where he discovered some of the Tongan group and the Hawaiian Islands, as well as Christmas Island.

See also:

The Golden Age of Exploration (volume 10, page 1372) • Southeast Asia (volume 7, page 972)

This jade pendant was made in New Zealand in the 18th century CE. Such pendants were passed down through the generations and were believed to accumulate the prestige of their owners.

TIME LINE

	SOUTHERN AND EASTERN ASIA	REST OF THE WORLD
	c. 38,000 BCE Humans first begin to inhabit Southeast Asia.	
	c. 30,000 BCE Lapita culture develops in New Guinea.	
		c. 17,000 BCE First nomadic Asian hunters enter Central America.
	c. 7500 BCE Jomon period begins in Japan.	
	c. 6000 BCE First farmers present in southern Asia.	c. 6000 BCE First farming settlements established in Greece and Crete.
c. 5000 BCE	c. 5000 BCE Emergence of Yang-shao culture in China.	c. 5000 BCE Semitic-speaking people move into Mesopotamia.
	c. 2600 BCE Earliest Indus Valley civilization develops.	
	c. 2200 BCE Establishment of first Chinese dynasty, the Xia.	c. 2100 BCE Migrants from central Asia arrive on Greek mainland.
	c. 1766 BCE Shang dynasty begins rule of Yellow River Valley.	
	c. 1500 BCE Aryans enter India from central Asia. First Vedas composed.	c. 1500 BCE Tumulus culture replaces Unetician culture in parts of Europe.
	1200 BCE Vedas first written down.	c. 1200 BCE Hallstatt culture emerges in present-day Austria.
	c. 1100 BCE Iron Age begins in India.	c. 1100 BCE Phoenicia establishes itself as dominant maritime power in Mediterranean.
	c. 1050 BCE Shang dynasty in China ousted by Zhou.	
	c. 1000 BCE Caste system emerges in India.	c. 1000 BCE Copper industry flourishes in southern Congo.

SOUTHERN AND EASTERN ASIA		REST OF THE WORLD	
c. 900 BCE	First Brahmanas composed as glosses to Vedas.	c. 900 BCE	Etruscan civilization develops in central Italy.
c. 800 BCE	Early Upanishads appended to Vedas.	c. 800 BCE	Poet Homer believed to have written *Iliad* and *Odyssey* around this time.
c. 570 BCE	Lao-tzu born.		
c. 563 BCE	Siddharta Gautama born.		
551 BCE	Kongqiu (known in West as Confucius) born.	539 BCE	Babylon falls to Persians.
c. 528 BCE	Siddharta becomes the Buddha.		
c. 500 BCE	Magadha becomes leading state in India. People of Dong Son culture begin to make bronze drums in Vietnam.	c. 500 BCE	Zapotec people become powerful in southern Mexico.
c. 490 BCE	Lao-tzu dies.	490 BCE	Persian forces defeated by Greeks at Battle of Marathon.
c. 483 BCE	The Buddha dies.		
479 BCE	Confucius dies.	479 BCE	Greek victory at Battle of Plataea effectively ends Persian Wars.
c. 475 BCE	Period of the Warring States begins in China.		
c. 383 BCE	Buddhists split into two factions at council in Vaishali.	387 BCE	Plato establishes Academy in Athens.
c. 371 BCE	Confucian philosopher Mencius born.	371 BCE	Thebes defeats Sparta at Battle of Leuctra.
321 BCE	Mauryan period begins in Magadha.		
268 BCE	Ashoka becomes emperor of India.	c. 300 BCE	Tiwanaku civilization begins to flourish in Andes.

c. 500 BCE

	SOUTHERN AND EASTERN ASIA		REST OF THE WORLD	
	c. 260 BCE	Ashoka converts to Buddhism.	260 BCE	Rome defeats Carthage at Battle of Mylae.
	c. 250 BCE	Jomon period ends in Japan; Yayoi period begins. Theravada Buddhism established in Ceylon.		
	221 BCE	Period of the Warring States ends. Shi Huang Di becomes first emperor of China at start of Qin dynasty.	216 BCE	Carthaginian general Hannibal inflicts massive defeat on Roman army at Battle of Cannae.
	213 BCE	Qin adopt legalism as state philosophy. Shi Huang Di orders burning of books.		
	206 BCE	Rebellion by Liu Bang leads to downfall of Qin dynasty and marks beginning of Han period.		
	204 BCE	Great Wall of China completed.		
c. 200 BCE	c. 200 BCE	Composition of Laws of Manu, early Hindu script.	c. 200 BCE	Germanic tribes begin moving southward, threatening borders of Roman Empire.
	185 BCE	Mauryan Empire ends in India; Shunga dynasty begins.		
	c. 140 BCE	Wu Ti becomes emperor of China; during his reign, Han dynasty reaches height of its power.		
	136 BCE	Han dynasty officially adopts Confucianism as Chinese state philosophy.	123 BCE	Roman politician Gaius Gracchus elected tribune; uses office to force social change.
	c. 110 BCE	China subjugates northern Vietnam, which becomes province of Annam.		

	SOUTHERN AND EASTERN ASIA		REST OF THE WORLD	
	c. 100 BCE	First Chinese historical work, *Shih-chi*, written.		
			44 BCE	Julius Caesar assassinated in senate on ides of March.
9 CE	**9 CE**	Wang Mang, a usurper, establishes short-lived Xin dynasty in China.	**9 CE**	Germanic tribes under Arminius inflict heavy defeat upon Romans in Teutoburg Forest.
	23 CE	Xin dynasty comes to end.		
	c. 100 CE	Inhabitants of Indonesia begin to migrate eastward and settle in Micronesia and Polynesia.		
	220 CE	Second Han period ends in China.	**c. 240 CE**	Prophet Mani has vision urging him to spread new religious faith.
	c. 320 CE	Gupta dynasty begins in India.		
	c. 400 CE	Hinduism develops into approximately modern form. First settlers arrive on Easter Island.	**c. 400 CE**	Ghana develops into empire.
	c. 500 CE	Buddhism established in China and Thailand.	**537 CE**	Hagia Sophia inaugurated in Constantinople.
	c. 550 CE	Buddhism imported to Japan from Korea.	**c. 550 CE**	Kiev emerges as leading city in Russia.
	618 CE	Tang period begins in China after overthrow of Sui dynasty.	**636 CE**	Bedouin warriors defeat Byzantine forces at Battle of Yarmuk River.
	c. 675 CE	Srivijaya kingdom starts to dominate maritime trade around Malay Archipelago in Southeast Asia.	**680 CE**	Battle of Karbala causes lasting rift between Shi'ite and Sunni Muslims.

	SOUTHERN AND EASTERN ASIA		REST OF THE WORLD
	702 CE	Japan adopts state system similar to that of China as result of Taika Reforms.		
	710 CE	Heijo becomes Japan's first fixed capital.	710 CE	Arabs capture Samarkand.
	711 CE	Arab forces attack Sind.		
	c. 750 CE	Pala dynasty begins in Bengal.	c. 750 CE	Teotihuacán is destroyed by fire in Mexico.
c. 800 CE	c. 800 CE	Khmer state begins to flourish in present-day Cambodia.	c. 800 CE	Maya from Guatemalan lowlands move to highlands and into Yucatán Peninsula. Chimú kingdom becomes powerful on coast of Peru. Polynesians settle in New Zealand.
	c. 1010 CE	*The Tale of Genji* written in Japan.		
	1024 CE	Muslim troops destroy Hindu temple at Somnath.		
	c. 1100 CE	Islamic conquest of northern India marginalizes region's Buddhists. Zen Buddhism established in Japan. In Cambodia, work begins on Khmer temple of Angkor Wat.	c. 1100 CE	First Incas settle in Cuzco Valley.
	1192 CE	Minamoto Yoritomo becomes shogun (military ruler) of Japan.	c. 1200 CE	Nomadic Mexica people settle on Lake Texcoco, a region dominated by Tepanecs. Anasazi complete settlement of Pueblo Bonito.
	1206 CE	Mamluk dynasty begins rule from Delhi.		
	1215 CE	Genghis Khan captures Yenking (modern Beijing).	1215 CE	English barons force King John to allow Magna Carta. Frederick II becomes Holy Roman emperor. Fourth Lateran Council outlaws trial by ordeal.
	1281 CE	Typhoon destroys Mongol force during attempted invasion of Japan.		

	SOUTHERN AND EASTERN ASIA		REST OF THE WORLD	
	1290 CE	Mamluk dynasty ends in Egypt.	c. 1300 CE	Anasazi and Mississippian peoples decline and disappear.
	1368 CE	Ming dynasty established in China.	c. 1382 CE	Moscow captured by Mongols of the Golden Horde.
	1398 CE	Mongols under leadership of Tamerlane attack Delhi.	c. 1400 CE	Hausa and Yoruba peoples dominate along Niger River. Aztecs oust Tepanecs as major power in Central America.
	c. 1450 CE	Malacca becomes first Southeast Asian state to adopt Islam.		
	1511 CE	Portuguese capture Malacca.		
1520 CE	1520 CE	Portuguese explorer Ferdinand Magellan becomes first European to enter Pacific Ocean.	1520 CE	Süleyman I takes power in Ottoman Empire; arts and culture flourish during his 46-year reign.
	1526 CE	Delhi Sultanate ends.	1532 CE	Spanish conquistador Francisco Pizarro conquers Inca Empire.
	1549 CE	Jesuit missionary Francis Xavier arrives in Japan; arrival leads to establishment of Christianity there.		
	1642 CE	Abel Tasman sights New Zealand.	1591 CE	Songhai conquered by Moroccans.
	1687 CE	Mughals conquer Golconda.	1644 CE	Manchu dynasty succeeds Ming dynasty in China.
	1722 CE	Jacob Roggeveen discovers Easter Island, so named because he arrived there on Easter Sunday.	1750 CE	Ashanti dominate central Ghana.
	1769 CE	James Cook arrives in Tahiti.		

GLOSSARY

Ahura Mazda Zoroastrian god of light and truth.

Ameratsu Japanese sun goddess from whom the imperial family claims direct descent.

Angkor Wat temple complex in Khmer capital; built around 1100 CE; famous monument in present-day Cambodia.

Aryans prehistoric inhabitants of Iran and northern India.

avatar from *avatara*, Sanskrit for "descent"; in Hinduism, the incarnation of a deity in human or animal form. The term usually refers to any of the 10 principal manifestations of the god Vishnu.

Brahma paramount Indian god; preacher of the Vedas; appears in Hinduism as part of the trinity of Brahma the creator, Vishnu the restorer, and Shiva the destroyer.

bronze copper-tin alloy widely used by 1700 BCE.

Bronze Age period during which bronze became the most important basic material; began around 3500 BCE in western Asia and around 1900 BCE in Europe.

Buddhism religion founded by Siddharta Gautama, called the Buddha; rejected much of Hinduism, including priestly authority, the Vedic scriptures, sacrificial practices, and the caste system. Its goal is nirvana (release from all desire and from the cycle of life, death and rebirth). The major schools of Buddhism are Theravada and Mahayana.

Cham Austronesian-speaking carvers and temple builders who prospered

until they were subdued by the Vietnamese in the 15th century CE.

Delhi Sultanate principal Muslim sultanate in northern India from 1206 to 1526 CE.

Dong Son culture that emerged around 2000 BCE; by 500 BCE, proficient in metallurgy and at producing distinctive bronze drums; named for a village in northern Vietnam where artifacts were first discovered.

Ezo northern part of Japan roughly coextensive with the island of Hokkaido.

Fujiwara period (858–1060 CE) era during which Japan was ruled by the Fujiwara family.

Ganesh Hindu god.

Great Wall of China defensive barrier that extended for 4,160 miles (6,700 km) along the country's northern and eastern frontiers; completed in 204 BCE.

Gupta Empire dynasty that ruled much of India (c. 320–550 CE) after a period of instability following the fall of the Mauryans.

Han dynasty ruling dynasty of China (206 BCE–220 CE); restored the agrarian economy and introduced Confucianism as the state religion; defeated the Huns and undertook expeditions across the Chinese borders. Government tasks were fulfilled by state officials from the class of large landowners called mandarins.

Heiji Disturbance confrontation in Japan in 1159 CE in which the Taira clan overcame the competing Minamoto clan. The Taira became

the major power in the land for a generation.

Heijo city in Nara that became Japan's first fixed capital in 710 CE. The capital had previously moved around with the emperor.

Hinduism predominant religion in India, originating from Brahmanism; characterized by belief in many gods headed by Brahma, Shiva, and Vishnu.

Homo erectus hominid who walked upright and lived between 500,000 and 150,000 years ago in Africa, Asia, and Europe; first hominid species to be found outside Africa; includes Java man (*Pithecanthropus*) and Peking man; used tools, made shelters, and utilized fires.

Huns central Asiatic people noted for horsemanship and ferocity in battle; drove the Visigoths from Ukraine (c. 370 CE); conquered eastern and central Europe in the fifth century CE; seized western Europe under Attila (c. 450 CE).

Hwang He (Hwang Ho; Yellow River) China's second longest river; flows for 3,395 miles (5,464 km) from the Plateau of Tibet to the Yellow Sea.

I Ching (Yi Jing; Book of Changes) Chinese divination manual; traditionally attributed to Confucius.

Indus river of south Asia that flows 1,800 miles (2,900 km) from southwestern Tibet to the Arabian Sea near modern Karachi (Pakistan).

iron metallic element (chemical symbol Fe) that can be made into tools, weapons, and ornaments. It is extracted from iron ore by heating and hammering it for long periods. Iron was being processed in Anatolia, western Asia, by 3000 BCE. Iron is easier to work with than bronze.

Iron Age period during which major tools and weapons were made of iron; followed the Bronze Age. The Hittites formed the first Iron Age culture around 1700 BCE. Between 1200 and 600 BCE, ironworking spread over Asia and Europe.

Jainism religion of India that teaches a path to spiritual purity and enlightenment through a disciplined mode of life founded on nonviolence to all living creatures; founded by Vardhamana (Mahavira) around the sixth century BCE.

Jomon period (c. 7500–250 BCE) early era of arts and crafts in Japan.

karma Sanskrit for "fate, work"; a person's acts and their consequences in a subsequent existence. In Buddhism, karma is considered the result of actions that define the kind of rebirth that occurs, not as punishment, but for evolution. In Hinduism, karma means cause and effect, bearing in this life the consequences of actions taken in previous lives.

Khmer ethnolinguistic group that emerged around 800 CE; now constitutes most of the population of Cambodia.

Lapita culture named after a site in New Guinea at which was found a type of fired pottery dating from around 30,000 BCE. The Lapita culture reached Fiji by around 1000 BCE.

Long-Shan (Lung-shan) Neolithic culture of central China (c. 2000–1850 BCE); named after the site in Shandong Province where its remains were first discovered.

Maurya major kingdom in India (c. 321–185 BCE). The Mauryan Empire reached the height of its power and

influence during the reign of Ashoka (ruled 268–233 BCE).

Ming dynasty Chinese dynasty (1368–1644 CE) under which the empire was extended substantially in all directions.

Mongols Asian tribes of horsemen who originally came from lands to the north of China; united by Genghis Khan in 1190 CE; conquered central Asian Islamic states, China, Russia, and the Delhi Sultanate in the 12th and 13th centuries CE.

Mughals Muslim dynasty that ruled India (1526–1857 CE); founded by Babur, a descendant of Genghis Khan.

Muslims worshippers of Allah; members of Islam.

Period of the Warring States last period (c. 475–221 BCE) of the Zhou (Chou) dynasty during which war was a constant fact of life, although trade, agriculture, and urbanization evolved simultaneously. Legislation and philosophy, such as Confucianism, legalism, and Taoism also developed at this time. At the end of the Period of Warring States, China was reunited.

Qin (Ch'in) dynasty rulers of northwestern China who took control of the whole country in 221 BCE. They established a central government and replaced the old feudal system with direct administration by officials.

samurai member of the Japanese warrior caste that rose to power in the 12th century CE and dominated the Japanese government until the Meiji Restoration in 1868 CE.

Shang dynasty the earliest Chinese dynasty (c. 1766–1050 BCE) of which there are documentary records. The main part of the realm was centrally governed while autonomous vassals were allowed to control outlying

areas. Most of the inhabitants were peasants who leased lands from the rulers in the cities and from the kings in exchange for labor.

Shintoism indigenous Japanese religion based on the worship of forefathers. The sun goddess, Ameratsu, the first mother, was the most prominent of the goddesses. The emperor was revered as her leading priest and her son.

Shiva Hindu god of destruction and reproduction; member of the Hindu trinity with Vishnu and Brahma; frequently manifests in female aspects, Parvati and Kali.

shogun originally the title given to the chief military commander of Japan; from 1192 CE, the hereditary title of honor for the emperor; continued to exist until 1868 CE.

Shu dynasty Chinese dynasty (221–263 CE) that rivaled the Han dynasty in southwestern China.

Silk Road ancient overland trade route that extended for 4,000 miles (6,400 km) and linked China and the West. First used as a caravan route, the road ran from Xi'an, China, along the Great Wall, through the Pamir Mountains, into Afghanistan, and on to the eastern Mediterranean Sea, where goods were taken onward by boat, mainly to Rome and Venice. On westbound journeys, the principal cargo was silk; wool, gold, and silver were the main commodities carried in the opposite direction.

Song (Sung) dynasty Chinese dynasty (960–1279 CE) that established its capital at Kaifeng in northern Henan (Honan) Province.

Spice Islands group of islands to the west of New Guinea; abundant source of cloves and nutmeg, which were highly desired as food flavorings by European countries and attracted western maritime traders of many nationalities, starting with the Portuguese in the early 16th century CE; present-day Moluccas.

Stone Age earliest period of human civilization, from around 2 million BCE to around 3500 BCE.

Taika Reforms period in Japan (645–702 CE) during which landownership was abolished and the power of the emperor's family was extended throughout society.

Taoism (Daoism) Chinese philosophy originated by Lao-tzu (Laozi) around 500 BCE; emphasizes inner harmony with nature and submission to the Tao (Dao; the Way).

uji Japanese clans forming a tribal society worshipping their own god. The emperor stood at the head of all clans, and political battles between clan leaders caused unrest.

Vedas the earliest sacred Hindu scriptures; four collections of sacrificial hymns taken over from oral tradition of Brahmanism and prescriptions for ritual; the *Rig-Veda*, the *Samaveda*, the *Yajurveda*, and the *Atharvaveda*.

Vishnu Hindu god called the preserver; forms a trinity with Brahma and Shiva; takes human form as Krishna.

Wu dynasty rival dynasty (222–280 CE) to the Han dynasty in the Yangtze River Valley.

Wu Jing (*Wu Ching*; *Five Classics*) five texts dated to the Zhou (Chou) dynasty (c. 600–500 BCE). According to tradition, they were edited or written by Confucius.

Xia (Hsia) dynasty China's first ruling dynasty; traditionally established by Yu the Great around 2200 BCE.

Xin dynasty short-lived Chinese dynasty (9–23 CE) founded by the usurper Wang Mang; ended during the chaos that followed a devastating change of course by the Yellow River.

Xi Xia (Hsi Hsia) Tangut tribe in northwestern China. They were paid annual tributes by the Song dynasty from 1044 CE.

Yamato Empire empire controlled by the *uji* (clan) of the sun goddess; made sun worship the state religion; controlled other Japanese *ujis* from the fifth century CE.

Yang-shao ancient Chinese farming and hunting culture (c. 5000–2000 BCE) that also made distinctive pottery without the use of wheels; named after the village in Henan (Honan) Province in which their relics were first discovered in the 20th century CE.

Yangtze world's third longest river; flows 3,400 miles (5,470 km) from the Plateau of Tibet to the East China Sea. Its fertile lower valley was the cradle of Chinese civilization.

Yayoi period era of Japanese history that lasted from around 250 BCE to the second or third century CE; characterized by the widespread practice of pottery and weaving and by the use of metal containers for the cultivation of rice.

Yin (Yinxu) capital of the late Shang dynasty; modern Anyang in Henan (Honan) Province. At its peak (c. 1250–1050 BCE), the city extended for 3.6 miles (5.8 km) along the Huan River.

yoga Sanskrit for "yoke"; Hindu school of philosophy and practice involving physical and mental discipline to restore and maintain the balance of spiritual energy; intense concentration attained by prescribed postures and exercises, including controlled breathing, to gain mystical union with Brahman.

Yüan dynasty Mongol dynasty established by Kublai Khan; ruled China from 1279 to 1368 CE.

Zen Buddhism Buddhist school originally developed in China, later in Japan; blending of Mahayana Buddhism and Taoism (Daoism).

Zhou (Chou) dynasty Chinese dynasty that ousted the Shang dynasty around 1050 BCE; ruled for almost a millennium until it was succeeded by the Qin (Ch'in) dynasty in 221 BCE.

Zoroastrianism traditional religion of Persians prior to conversion to Islam; founded by Zoroaster; posited competing spirits of good and evil.

MAJOR HISTORICAL FIGURES

Ashoka Mauryan emperor who ruled between 268 and 233 BCE; contributed to the spread of Buddhism across India.

Bindusara Mauryan emperor between around 293 and 268 BCE; extended his power far into southern India; father of Ashoka.

Cai Lun (Ts'ai Lun) Chinese court eunuch; traditionally credited as the first maker of paper, in 105 CE.

Chandragupta Maurya founder of the Mauryan Empire and conqueror of the Indus Valley; ruled between around 321 and 293 BCE.

Columbus, Christopher (1451–1506 CE) Genoese mariner who discovered the New World in 1492 CE.

Confucius (Kongqiu; K'ung) (551–479 BCE) Chinese philosopher and founder of Confucianism.

Genghis Khan (c. 1162–1227 CE) first leader to unite the Mongols, whom he led on a campaign of conquest that took in China and some Islamic empires.

Go-Sanjo first Japanese emperor in more than a century not to be related to the Fujiwaras; ruled between 1060 and 1073 CE.

Han Fei (Han-fei-tzu) (died 233 BCE) Chinese legalist philosopher whose works exerted a major influence on the development of autocratic government.

Iname Japanese emperor of the Soga clan; ruled between 536 and 570 CE; early sponsor of Buddhism.

Kalidasa Indian poet and dramatist; wrote in Sanskrit. His dates are uncertain, but he probably lived during the reign of the Gupta king Chandragupta II, who ruled between 375 and 414 CE.

Kammu Japanese emperor who ruled between 781 and 806 CE; moved the capital to Heian-kyo (present-day Kyoto).

Kanishka king of the Kushan dynasty; ruled between around 100 and 130 CE; outstanding patron of Buddhism.

Kublai Khan Mongolian general and statesman; grandson of Genghis Khan; ruled between 1260 and 1294 CE. He conquered China and became the first emperor of its Yüan, or Mongol, dynasty. In that role, he promoted the integration of Chinese and Mongol civilizations.

Lao-tzu (Laozi) (c. 570–490 BCE) Chinese philosopher whose ideas are recorded in the *Tao Te Ching* (*Dao De Jing*; *Classic of the Way and Its Virtue*).

Li Si (Li Ssu) (c. 280–208 BCE) Chinese statesman and philosopher; used his political theories to unite the warring states into the centralized Qin (Ch'in) dynasty (221–206 BCE).

Liu Bang (Liu Pang) army officer of nonaristocratic birth who proclaimed the Han dynasty in 206 BCE.

Magellan, Ferdinand (1480–1521 CE) Portuguese navigator who began the first circumnavigation of the world.

Mencius (Mengzi) (c. 371–289 BCE) early Chinese philosopher who developed orthodox Confucianism.

Minamoto Yoritomo shogun ruler of Japan between 1192 and 1199 CE.

Muhammad ibn Tughluq sultan who briefly extended the rule of the Delhi Sultanate of northern India over most of the subcontinent; ruled between 1325 and 1351 CE.

Shi Huang Di (Shi Huang Ti) regional ruler who declared himself emperor of China and founded the Qin (Ch'in) dynasty; emperor between 221 and 210 BCE.

Siddharta Gautama (c. 563–483 BCE) Nepalese holy man and teacher; founder of Buddhism.

Sima Yan (Ssu-ma Yen) emperor of China; seized the throne in 265 CE, establishing the Jin (Ching) dynasty; reunited the north and south of the country by 280 CE. The dynasty remained stable until 290 CE.

Tamerlane (Timur the Lame) Mongolian ruler between around 1369 and 1405 CE; subjected the Mongols in the west; conquered territory in Persia, India, Syria; spread Islam.

Vima Kadphises Kushan emperor who conquered the Indus Valley and much of the Gangetic Plain; ruled between around 75 and 100 CE.

Wang Mang government official who overthrew the Han dynasty and founded the short-lived Xin dynasty; ruled between 9 and 23 CE.

Xavier, Francis (1506–1552 CE) first Jesuit missionary to establish Christianity in Japan.

Zhao Kuangyin (Chao K'uang-yin) Chinese general who seized the throne in 960 CE and declared himself the first Song (Sung) emperor.

RESOURCES FOR FURTHER STUDY

BOOKS

Berinstain, Valerie. *India and the Mughal Dynasty*. New York, 1998.

Bhargava, P.L. *Chandragupta Maurya*. Lucknow, India, 1935.

Bhaskarananda, Swami. *The Essentials of Hinduism: A Comprehensive Overview of the World's Oldest Religion*. Seattle, WA, 2002.

Blofeld, John. *Taoism: The Road to Immortality*. Boulder, CO, 1978.

Boozer, Celina LuZanne. *Heritage of Buddha: The Story of Siddhartha Gautama*. New York, 1953.

Confucius (translated by Arthur Waley). *The Analects of Confucius*. New York, 1989.

Cotterell, Arthur. *Ancient China*. New York, 2005.

Deedrick, Tami. *Khmer Empire*. Austin, TX, 2002.

Drews, Robert. *The End of the Bronze Age: Changes in Warfare and the Catastrophe ca. 1200 B.C.* Princeton, NJ, 1993.

Eaton, Richard M. *India's Islamic Traditions, 711–1750*. New Delhi, India, 2003.

Eraly, Abraham. *The Mughal Throne: The Saga of India's Great Emperors*. London, England, 2003.

Fisher, Leonard Everett. *The Great Wall of China*. New York, 1986.

Flood, Gavin D. *An Introduction to Hinduism*. New York, 1996.

Gascoigne, Bamber. *The Dynasties of China: A History*. New York, 2003.

Habu, Junko. *Ancient Jomon of Japan*. New York, 2004.

Han, Fei. *Han Fei Tzu: Basic Writings*. New York, 1964.

Hardy, Grant. *The Establishment of the Han Empire and Imperial China*. Westport, CT, 2005.

Hirth, Friedrich. *The Ancient History of China, to the End of the Chou Dynasty*. Freeport, NY, 1969.

Iggulden, Conn. *Genghis: Birth of an Empire*. New York, 2007.

Ingram, Scott. *The Song Dynasty*. San Diego, CA, 2004.

Jackson, Peter. *The Delhi Sultanate: A Political and Military History*. New York, 1999.

Jansma, Rudi. *Introduction to Jainism*. Jaipur, India, 2006.

Kalidasa. *Complete Works of Kalidasa*. Thrissur, India, 2000.

Kirch, Patrick Vinton. *The Lapita Peoples: Ancestors of the Oceanic World*. Cambridge, MA, 1997.

Knott, Kim. *Hinduism: A Very Short Introduction*. New York, 2000.

Kramer, Sydelle. *Who Was Ferdinand Magellan?* New York, 2004.

Kure, Mitsuo. *Samurai: An Illustrated History*. Boston, MA, 2002.

Laozi (translated by Ni Hua-Ching). *Complete Works of Lao Tzu*. Malibu, CA, 1979.

Lewis, Mark Edward. *The Early Chinese Empires: Qin and Han*. Cambridge, MA, 2007.

Loewe, Michael. *The Government of the Qin and Han Empires: 221 BCE–220 CE*. Indianapolis, IN, 2006.

Marozzi, Justin. *Tamerlane: Sword of Islam, Conqueror of the World*. London, England, 2004.

Mason, R.H.P. *A History of Japan*. New York, 1974.

Mookerji, Radhakumud. *Chandragupta Maurya and His Times*. Delhi, India, 1966.

———. *The Gupta Empire*. Delhi, India, 1969.

Morgan, David. *The Mongols*. Malden, MA, 2007.

Novesky, Amy. *The Elephant Prince: The Story of Ganesh*. San Rafael, CA, 2004.

Ortner, Jon. *Angkor: Celestial Temples of the Khmer Empire.* New York, 2002.

Pavan, Aldo. *Yellow River: The Spirit and Strength of China.* New York, 2007.

Possehl, Gregory L. *The Indus Civilization: A Contemporary Perspective.* Walnut Creek, CA, 2002.

Rightmire, G. Philip. *The Evolution of Homo Erectus: Comparative Anatomical Studies of an Extinct Human Species.* New York, 1990.

Rossabi, Morris. *Khubilai Khan: His Life and Times.* Berkeley, CA, 1988.

Rudgley, Richard. *The Lost Civilizations of the Stone Age.* New York, 1999.

Sansom, George Bailey. *A History of Japan* (three volumes). Stanford, CA, 1958–1963.

Sawyer, Ralph D. *The Art of the Warrior: Leadership and Strategy from the Chinese Military Classics: With Selections from the Seven Military Classics of Ancient China and Sun Pin's Military Methods.* Boston, MA, 1996.

———. *Fire and Water: The Art of Incendiary and Aquatic Warfare in China.* Boulder, CO, 2003.

Seagrave, Sterling. *The Yamato Dynasty: The Secret History of Japan's Imperial Family.* New York, 1999.

Singh, Lalan Prasad. *Zen Buddhism.* New York, 1988.

Smith, Huston. *Buddhism: A Concise Introduction.* New York, 2003.

Smith, Vincent Arthur. *Asoka: The Buddhist Emperor of India.* Delhi, India, 1964.

Storl, Wolf-Dieter. *Shiva: The Wild God of Power and Ecstasy.* Rochester, VT, 2004.

Talreja, Kanayalal M. *Holy Vedas and Holy Bible: A Comparative Study.* New Delhi, India, 2000.

Taylor, Philip. *Cham Muslims of the Mekong Delta: Place and Mobility in the Cosmopolitan Periphery.* Honolulu, HI, 2007.

Thakur, Manoj K. *India in the Age of Kanishka.* Delhi, India, 1999.

Thompson, E.A. *The Huns.* Cambridge, MA, 1996.

Thorp, Robert L. *China in the Early Bronze Age: Shang Civilization.* Philadelphia, PA, 2006.

Thubron, Colin. *Shadow of the Silk Road.* New York, 2007.

Thubten Chodron. *Buddhism for Beginners.* Ithaca, NY, 2001.

Underwood, Alfred Clair. *Shintoism: The Indigenous Religion of Japan.* London, England, 1934.

Van Over, Raymond (ed.). *I Ching.* New York, 1971.

Weatherford, J. McIver. *Genghis Khan and the Making of the Modern World.* New York, 2004.

Yamashita, Michael S. *The Great Wall: From Beginning to End.* New York, 2007.

WEB SITES

Ahura Mazda
Article on the Zoroastrian god of light and truth; includes links to several topics of related interest
http://www.livius.org/ag-ai/ahuramazda/ahuramazda.html

Ancient China
Web site that contains photographs of a number of ancient Chinese artifacts as well as a variety of interactive features
http://www.ancientchina.co.uk/menu.html

Angkor Wat
Web site that includes a wealth of photographs of the Cambodian temple complex
http://whc.unesco.org/en/list/668

Aryans
Web site that discusses the true origins of these mysterious and influential Asian people
http://www.iranchamber.com/history/articles/aryan_people_origins.php

Babur
Web site that is devoted to the life and times of the first Mughal emperor
http://www.bbc.co.uk/religion/religions/islam/history/mughalempire_2.shtml

Borobudur
Account of the discovery of the vast Buddhist temple on the island of Java
http://www.pbs.org/treasuresoftheworld/a_nav/boro_nav/main_borofrm.html

RESOURCES FOR FURTHER STUDY

Brahma
Web site that describes the functions and significance of one of the principal Hindu deities
http://www.sanatansociety.org/hindu_gods_and_goddesses/brahma.htm

Buddhism
Web site that provides a comprehensive outline of Buddhist beliefs
http://www.bbc.co.uk/religion/religions/buddhism

Genghis Khan
Web site that describes the journey of the Mongol leader from his native land to the gates of Vienna.
http://www.fsmitha.com/h3/h11mon.htm

Great Wall of China
Web site that provides information about the wall's construction and history
http://www.travelchinaguide.com/china_great_wall

Gupta Empire
Web site that gives the historical background of the empire and supplies links to information about other civilizations
http://www.wsu.edu/~dee/ANCINDIA/GUPTA.HTM

Hinduism
Web site that provides a comprehensive outline of Hindu beliefs
http://www.bbc.co.uk/religion/religions/hinduism

Huns
Web site that describes the origins of the Asian people and their influence on Europe
http://www.imninalu.net/Huns.htm

Jainism
Web site that provides a comprehensive outline of Jainist beliefs
http://www.bbc.co.uk/religion/religions/jainism

Khmer Culture
Web site that is dedicated to the culture of ancient Cambodia; contains articles about the restoration of Angkor Wat and other relevant archaeological projects
http://www.khmerculture.net

Ming Dynasty
Web site that covers the most important aspects of the era and provides links to articles about other Chinese imperial periods
http://www.mnsu.edu/emuseum/prehistory/china/later_imperial_china/ming.html

Mongols
Web site that gives a detailed and highly illustrated account of the individuals and policies that turned the steppe nomads into the lords of the largest Eurasian empire in history
http://afe.easia.columbia.edu/mongols

Mughals
Web site about the dynasty that ruled India in the 16th and 17th centuries CE
http://www.wsu.edu/~dee/MUGHAL/CONTENTS.HTM

Yangtze River
Web site that provides details about the longest river in Asia
http://cgee.hamline.edu/rivers/Resources/river_profiles/Yangtze.html

Yellow River
Web site that deals with every aspect of the river, from its physical dimensions to its psychological effect on Chinese life and culture
http://www.cis.umassd.edu/~gleung

INDEX